# The Church Women Want

*Catholic Women
in Dialogue*

Edited by
ELIZABETH A. JOHNSON

*A Herder & Herder Book*
The Crossroad Publishing Company
New York

The Crossroad Publishing Company
481 Eighth Avenue, New York, NY 10001

Printed in the United States of America

Library of Congress Cataloging-in-Publication Data

The church women want : Catholic women in dialogue / edited by Elizabeth
    A. Johnson.
        p. cm.
    "A Herder & Herder book."
    Includes bibliographical references.
    ISBN 0-8245-1979-5
    1. Women in the Catholic Church—Congresses. 2. Catholic
women—Religious life—Congresses. I. Johnson, Elizabeth A., 1941-
BX2347.8.W6 C487 2002
282'.082—dc21

                                                          2002006048

        3    4    5    6    7    8    9    10    06    05    04

# Contents

# Introduction

ELIZABETH A. JOHNSON
*and*
CATHERINE M. PATTEN

S HORTLY BEFORE HE DIED, Cardinal Joseph Bernardin of Chicago
founded the Catholic Common Ground Initiative to promote
dialogue about critical issues in the church. The charter statement
reads in part: "There are urgent questions that the church in the
United States knows it must air openly and honestly but which it
increasingly feels pressed to evade or, at best, address obliquely.
These issues include: the changing roles of women," followed by
other concerns such as eucharistic liturgy, sexuality, formation of
lay ministers, responsibility to the poor, cultural diversity, and
decision making in church governance.[1] In place of the polarization and partisan attacks that seem to be gripping the church, the
Initiative calls for these problems to be engaged through "constructive debate" by persons of different viewpoints. There is no
need to fudge or water down distinctive visions. When these are
expressed in a dialogue conducted in an atmosphere of mutual
respect, all parties can listen, learn, contribute, wrestle with the
insights, and be tested and refined. The process is healthy and ultimately builds up a vital future for the church.

Two Catholic women's colleges in New York, Marymount College in Tarrytown and the College of New Rochelle, took up this
challenge to dialogue. In cooperation with the Catholic Common

Ground Initiative they planned a symposium on women and the church that met on four Sunday afternoons stretching over the two years that ushered in the new millennium. To open up a wide scope for dialogue, they announced as the overarching theme: "What kind of church are American Catholic women looking toward in the twenty-first century?" The sessions, moderated by Margaret O'Brien Steinfels, who is editor of the journal *Commonweal*, addressed in turn women's spirituality, embodiment and the difference it makes, racism as it affects and divides women, and women as agents of change in church and society. For each session, women of differing views presented a brief position paper intended to start the conversation among the hundreds in attendance. These are the papers gathered in this book.

From the outset the planners desired to provide space and time in the program to "give voice" to the women who came. Thus, each Sunday afternoon symposium featured a similar format. Presentations by two or three panelists were followed by a short dialogue between or among them. Then the participants, seated randomly in table groups with a facilitator, engaged in their own dialogue to plumb and to share what they had seen and heard and felt and thought. The facilitator at each table gathered questions or comments for Steinfels, who used them to focus a final conversation among the presenters from all four sessions. Most of the presenters, despite multiple commitments, were present for all the sessions. The original invitation had asked the participants also to commit themselves to be present for all four sessions in the hope that the dialogue would deepen over time. Comments after the last session affirmed that "people got better at the dialogue process" and that "the experiences of the process and discussion meaningfully built on each other." However, a recurring concern was that such a long-term commitment "may have prevented some people from coming."

Above all, the women's commitment to participate for two years spoke eloquently of their desire for such an exchange. When asked what drew them to the symposium, some highlighted the content, for example, "I come to have my mind opened and to be informed," "I come because I know I'll be exposed to thinkers/ theologians (female, Catholic) who are on top of current thinking. Wouldn't get this anywhere else." Others spoke of personal frustration with the way things were: "What draws me is being a woman who knows the need for change in the church. I can either belong and wait while I turn blue or make the steps, however slow, towards change."

The symposium was not widely advertised. Invitations were sent to alumnae/friends of the two colleges and to those on the Initiative mailing list from the New York metropolitan area. Consequently the approximately 250 people who came were relatively homogeneous—mostly women, religious and lay, well-educated, white, middle-class, and middle-aged and older. Table facilitators reported that many of these women expressed disappointment that their hopes for greater voice and inclusion after Vatican II had not been realized. A survey of participants' ages and occupations revealed that almost all were engaged in church-related work, such as teaching or administration in Catholic institutions; or in work inspired by their faith, such as social-service programs with the poor or United Nations non-governmental agencies.

After each session the participants themselves looked around the room and lamented the absence of younger women, more conservative women, and women of color. The audience, therefore, did not reflect the diversity of the presenters, and it predictably preferred the more "liberal" perspective articulated each time. Nonetheless, many participants expressed appreciation in each session's evaluations for the intellectual challenge, for having been prodded to hear another view and to consider the complexity of an issue.

*Called to Be Catholic*, the charter statement of the Initiative, asserts: "Ultimately, the fresh eyes and changed hearts we need cannot be distilled from guidelines. They emerge in the space created by praise and worship." Thus, the symposium took place in the context of worship. Participants were invited to begin each day together by celebrating Eucharist with the College of New Rochelle community, and each session concluded with evening prayer.

Was the original question answered: What kind of church are American Catholic women looking toward in the twenty-first century? Was "common ground" articulated or achieved? Certainly participants endorsed no statements, nor did they approve any set of propositions. The group seemed more interested in opening up questions than in pinning down answers. But it may be truer to say that their *actions*—returning for all four sessions and engaging earnestly in the dialogue with others—embodied their concerns: they want to be taken seriously, to be able to contribute their gifts in the church community, to build bridges across contemporary divides, to develop ways of speaking and listening. These are women who experience their dignity and worth in other arenas and whose pain at being "marginalized in the church"—an expression they themselves used—by contrast, is palpable. One woman spoke of her "wrestling with the issue of women and church as raised to and for me by my twenty-two- and twenty-six-year-old daughters." A man who attended summed up the session: "American women—women all over the world—have a lot to offer the church. They feel their offer is not being accepted." These are women who have remained active in the church because they care so deeply about their faith and tradition. As an eighty-three-year-old retired lawyer put it, she came because of her "love for the church and interest in the equality of women."

In the first dialogue, Susan Muto focused her reflections on the relationship of solitude and solidarity in the Christian life, especially in the vocation to the single life. She described "spiritual friendship" as the bridge between personal contemplative union with Christ and the call to co-labor "as persons called to be one in Christ Jesus to fulfill the pastoral mission of the Church." In contrast, Miriam Therese Winter saw her Christian commitment as leading to a global, cosmic horizon and a radical feminist commitment to the liberation of all peoples of every culture, class, race, and religion. She described an inclusive vision that stretches boundaries even to the breaking point, while Muto's vision was carefully bounded by the church's tradition and understanding of its mission.

Yet a telling moment occurred when they had trouble with their microphones. Winter turned spontaneously to Muto, took her by the hand, and led her to the podium. Muto responded with humor and grace. They held hands, smiling, and continued their dialogue at a shared microphone. The audience erupted with glee. The presenters' embodiment of dialogue, mutual respect, humor, and willingness to speak their truth and to listen to one another across significant differences imaged what most participants wanted.

The second session, "Embodiment: Women and Men, Equal or Complementary?" struck different chords. The program, originally bringing into dialogue two theologians with strong disagreements about whether women can image Christ, an underlying issue in the church's position against the ordination of women, shifted when one of the presenters, Elizabeth Johnson, fell ill and was unable to come. In this volume, the balance is somewhat redressed with the inclusion of her written essay. At the symposium, Colleen Griffith advocated an approach that begins with our common humanity and sees gender difference as secondary. Her presentation started not with the traditional theological categories and debates, but with an attempt to recast the question using insights from the social sciences. It created an asymmetry between her arguments and Sr. Sara Butler's. Butler recast the classical position on the complementarity of men and women into a framework proposed by Pope John Paul II. A number of participants expressed gratitude for the clarity of her presentation. As one participant put it, "I did not agree with Sara Butler but was deep down pleased to hear someone trying to put forth and forward his [Pope John Paul II's] teaching."

Others asked that such theologizing be given a clearly practical side. A hospital trustee spoke of dealing with an "old boys'" network, changing roles of health care, and difficult finances" and asked "Where is there Christian Catholic discussion on serious issues like these? Real body stuff." Another commented, "The reproductive function of human beings is exercised for a short period of a person's life and does not define the totality or more important aspect of a person. Brains, for example, are more important than the genitals." Participants at several of the table groups asked why a gap exists between the church's teaching about women's dignity and equality and what is often their experience in the church. Several others asked how the schema of male/female relationships deals with nontraditional families.

The third session shifted to the question, What unites and divides us as women? Presenter Barbara Andolsen, a white feminist ethicist, challenged the audience to become aware of white privilege and to assume the God-given task of asking why so many children of Hispanic and black women are suffering and dying. Diana Hayes delivered a ringing call to be aware of the double oppression suffered by black women in this church and country, while Ana María Díaz-Stevens appealed to all present to move beyond fear and stereotypes to create a culture and church that mirror our unity in the Body of Christ.

In some ways culture and race were the most divisive issues, with the participants' perspectives clearly shaped by their life experiences. When Barbara Andolsen suggested in the final dialogue that our understandings of what is "civil discourse" may be culturally conditioned, others in the room protested vociferously. Mary Ann Glendon asserted, and others agreed, that civil discourse is essential in any exploration of common ground. But Andolsen was suggesting that assumptions about what constitutes civil discourse are culturally conditioned. Others acknowledged that the questions posed by the symposium were those of white women, and they wondered aloud whether women of color might have proposed and responded to different issues. The common ground in this session was shared good will and an increased awareness of how difficult, painful, and culturally conditioned such issues are. During the two years, the participants regularly observed that they were too homogeneous—socially, ethnically, and racially, as well in experience and age. The tensions the group experienced around race and ethnicity, however, illustrated the power of culture in one's experience of church, a point the presenters were making.

That experience was reinforced when Mary Ann Glendon invited a group of younger women from Regnum Christi, a lay movement, to attend the fourth session. Although they were mostly white, middle-class women, they brought a different and "more conservative" view of church and society to the conversation. Most, although not all, of the participants welcomed their challenge. As one participant said, "Having younger people (including students) present at this last session really made a positive impact." Congresswoman Marcy Kaptur and Mary Ann Glendon approached their topic, "Women as Leaven in Church and Society," from sharply different stances. One table group reported that it was "Kaptured" by Marcy Kaptur's ringing call for women to participate in church decision making. She had done what many women would like the church to do more often—consulted large numbers of women, solicited their views, and reported her findings. Kaptur confessed that she was "astonished"—she who has authority to vote on billion-dollar appropriations in Congress—that even women invited to observe a meeting of U.S. bishops have no voice or vote. Clearly the audience resonated with her consternation. Kaptur distinguished between ordination and participation in church decision making, saying that she had learned that the people who make budgetary decisions wield the real power in any organization.

In contrast, Mary Ann Glendon held a global perspective, raising up the positive contribution the church has made to women's dignity and rights in many countries down through the centuries and also today. Glendon began by asserting that all Christians have no choice but to be leaven. She noted that many women who have had successful careers in business have become part of the corporate culture; they have not changed it. Her query, "Are we more American than Catholic?" clearly struck a chord: many of the small groups took it as a focus of their dialogue and reported that they recognized the challenge of the question. Glendon affirmed and asked for support for women who choose to give parenting priority over careers, and she raised up the example of Dorothy Day as a "saint for the twenty-first century."

For some who came, such a dialogue itself was a first: "It was tremendously valuable to hear other women talking about their relationship with God and their concerns about the church. It is not something I ever had an opportunity to experience before." One young student from a rural state, here visiting a friend, mused that "a group of women of this caliber, giving both sides of the issue, is a rarity in my hometown. This is an amazing opportunity." The process got all participants thinking about their beliefs and views. All were grateful for the opportunity to hear other voices. Many in turn dared to speak, being "heard into speech" by the attentive listening of others.[2] The consequences were personally enriching: people felt challenged, stimulated, empowered, heartened, and refreshed. They resolved to do more for women, to harness their anger constructively, and to grow in commitment along with other women who care about the church. They especially desired to bring young women into the conversation, since the future rests largely in their hands. For all the differences expressed, there was yet a further dissenting view: "I'd be happier if the presenters were more diverse in their views. Can we get Mother Angelica?"

These brief papers or discussion starters are made public as a way of extending this crucial conversation. Read their diversity of views and discover the common ground that emerges. Add your own points of view. Use them as they are or as models to stage yet further dialogue sessions. In the process, hope will keep bubbling up despite the present tensions. From this point on there can be no future for the church that women have not had a pivotal hand in shaping. Women are silent and invisible no longer.

## NOTES

1. *Called to Be Catholic: Church in a Time of Peril,* available from the National Pastoral Life Center, 18 Bleecker St., New York, NY 10012. Phone 212-431-7825. Online at www.nplc.org

2. "Hearing each other into speech" is the often-used phrase of Nelle Morton, *The Journey Is Home* (Boston: Beacon, 1985).

# Part 1

## Women and Spirituality/ Worship

A T THE VERY HEART of the church's life of faith lies the relationship of individuals and the community as a whole to the loving mystery of God. One might expect that this matter of spirituality, expressed in personal prayer, public worship, and acting according to gospel values would not be a zone of controversy. As women come to voice, however, they express real differences. Some are basically content in the present arrangement, seeking mainly greater respect for and use of women's diverse gifts in the church. Others express gnawing hunger for the sacred. Their deep spiritual needs are not being met by current institutional administration of word and sacrament. Therefore, making the distinction between spirituality and religion, they seek God together in new ways. Susan Muto expounds the first perspective, creatively pairing solitude before God and solidarity with others in imitation of Christ, the ground of all spirituality. Living this way gives impetus to fostering greater genuine collaboration between men in hierarchical office and women in the church. Miriam Therese Winter, by contrast, gives voice to an explicitly feminist spirituality growing among those who are exploring women's religious experience within and beyond the framework of the institutional church. Finding deep personal liberation plus a call to justice on this path, they argue for a church more open to the Spirit. This would entail inclusive language for humans as well as for the images and names used of God; women's liturgical leadership in preaching and celebrating the Eucharist; and women's participation in decision making in all areas of church governance.

9

Common ground developed as both agreed that women's religious experience must be attended to as a source for a spirituality that is deeply rooted and contemplative. This agreement in difference took moving visual form as one reached for the hand of the other when they stood to answer questions. Common ground emerged in the clasp of a sister's hand.

Hearing each other into speech, circles of women expressed their own insights. Some appreciated the idea of collaborative friendship between women and men. Others expressed concern that without analysis this idea could nicely veil male dominance. Some are not disturbed by the failure to ordain women; they do not feel the need for this exercise of authority. Many more were "tremendously frustrated" and "heartsick" over what they perceive to be the injustice of the official church's position and argued for radical change in church structures. Virtually all wished to extend this conversation to the bishops, though there was doubt whether at this point church leaders would take women's concerns seriously. This, perhaps, was the most poignant note struck as women discussed their lives in relationship to God.

— E. J.

# 1

## Called to Holiness
## as Women of the Church

### SUSAN MUTO

C HRISTIAN SPIRITUALITY IS THE ART and discipline of bringing
Christ into the here-and-now reality of our daily lives. The
two faces of this call are clear: one is unique, the other communal.
One draws us to solitude, as when Jesus goes off to a lonely place
to pray (Matt. 14:23), the other to solidarity with others in need, as
when Jesus feeds the five thousand (Matt. 14:21).

Both dynamics, lived in a balanced and creative way, in fidelity
to our vocation, enable us to respond in a fully human and graced
way to the universal call to holiness. We thereby proclaim by our
lives as laity, clergy, and religious, as single and married members
of the church, the Good News of Jesus Christ. Jesus operated not
from the authority of righteousness vested in the ruling empire or
the religious elite, but from the authority of holiness vested in the
House of David. He shunned the paths of power, pleasure, and
possession and chose instead the ways of obedience, chastity, and
poverty. He reveals the great paradoxes that in powerlessness
resides true power; that in respect for every person—tax collectors
and prostitutes, merchants and street people—lies real love; and
that in sharing what we have we receive more than we could possibly give.

The Christocentric models of singularity and collaborative

11

sharing or solidarity provide the framework for the two issues I wish to discuss. In my mind they touch upon the ground on which we dare to walk in common: our respect for human life and dignity in its splendid uniqueness (no two fingerprints are alike) and in its equally splendid longing for union with God and communion with others.

In exploring the kind of church American Catholic women and men look toward in the twenty-first century and in reflecting specifically on women and spirituality with a view toward worship, I must return in time to what was perhaps the most significant experience of church in my life at the end of the twentieth century. This was the period from 1984 to 1992—a span of nine years—during which I served as the principal writer for the committee tasked by the National Conference of Catholic Bishops (NCCB) to draft a pastoral letter on women's concerns for church and society. While this letter as such, even after four major published drafts, failed to achieve unanimous approval by the body of bishops, its concluding twenty-five action items—thanks I might add to the remarkable reconciling intervention of Cardinal Bernardin—were approved as part of the committee report. I see their fruits at work even today in such documents as the 1994 pastoral reflection *Strengthening the Bonds of Peace* and in the 1998 statement of the NCCB committee on women in society and the church entitled *From Words to Deeds: Continuing Reflections on the Role of Women in the Church.*

Strong statements condemning violence against women, upholding women's dignity, and reexamining the role of women in the church in decision making and other ministerial positions open to the laity can in many ways be traced to the original work of the pastoral committee in listening to the testimonies of women and responding to them in the light of our faith and formation tradition. I have found myself of late returning every so often to the first published draft of the pastoral entitled, appropriately enough, *Partners in the Mystery of Redemption* (1988). Both of the issues I wish to discuss—the need to make more visible in word and symbol the place and role of single women and consecrated virgins in the church of the new millennium and the need to promote and foster genuine collaboration for the good of the church between women and men equally committed to prayer and service—took root during that long gestation period of writing and rewriting four published drafts of the pastoral.

I was able to make a personal contribution to the first topic because of my own call and commitment to the single life. I learned from the hundreds of reports we received from dioceses around the country that especially women single by choice or by circumstance (for example, separated, divorced, widowed, or in transition to marriage) and consecrated virgins, living their vocation in the world or as women religious in community, found theirs to be an often marginalized or increasingly questioned vocation in the church. To address this concern in my own life, I wrote *Celebrating the Single Life* (1982), in which I focused on singleness not as a negative (not being married) but as a unique vocation and a call to discipleship that enables one to walk in a special way in the footsteps of Christ, who was and remained a single person in the world.

Here are a few lines from *Partners in the Mystery of Redemption* (§92) that to this day need more dialogue and implementation if their intention is to be realized:

> While the vocation to religious life has long been honored by the Church, the problems and concerns of single women are only recently receiving attention in preaching and pastoral care. Yet the single way of life is given full recognition in the Scriptures (cf. 1 Corinthians 7:25–40; 1 Timothy 5:3–16)—a recognition we affirm and seek to restore.
>
> Women who are single by choice or circumstance, whether unmarried, widowed, or divorced, constitute a large and important sector of the church. Single life is an occasion for solitude and solidarity. It represents freedom from certain responsibilities so that one can be free for other cares that are just as fruitful and necessary. This calling is remarkably creative when it is lived in chastity and service to others. The single life is rich in personal development and achievement, in friendship and contemplation. Today many single people are engaged in the church's struggle for social justice

and their efforts should be supported. As bishops we deeply appreciate the beauty and holiness to be found in the single members of our local churches, who contribute greatly to its life and ministry. Therefore, we urge all people, especially pastors, to show their appreciation and gratitude to the single members of their parish.

The continuation of a climate conducive to the single life for women will be specifically enhanced by appropriate economic freedom, a diversity of professional choices, and a mature appreciation of each person's limits and strengths. Single persons face many challenges morally and spiritually, yet with God's grace their vocation can be lived in the world in fidelity to Christ, their model, and in keeping with the tenets of our Catholic tradition.

A key word in this text is *friendship*. In fact, I believe it is the best word around which to build a bridge between my first and second concern. In a word, that second concern is for collaboration, which means literally co-laboring or striving together as persons called to be one in Christ Jesus to fulfill the pastoral mission of the church.

Different opinions abound as to how to foster the single vocation or how to promote the necessity of collaboration, but the common ground on which both solitude and solidarity rest is the recognition that Christ himself perfectly lived both of these elements. It was out of his single-hearted love for the Father that he embraced the community of disciples and set the church on the path of unity and diversity she must continue to pursue in the coming era. I cannot emphasize enough the latter word, for in many ways diversity is the face of divinity as seen in the enormous number of people of every race and nation who gather under the motherly wings of the church. Her walls are made more of rubber than of cement when it comes to embracing Catholics who are Caucasian, Asian, African, Hispanic, or Indian. The list is as diverse as the ecology of the earth and yet as unified as the mystery of the Eucharist.

I experienced a glimpse of the church of the future in its unity and multiplicity during those long days and often nights of work on the pastoral, a labor I shared with the members of the writing committee, one of whom was Sr. Sara Butler. The six bishops

assigned to see the project through from start to finish became
mentors and friends to us all. We learned, among other things, how
to disagree agreeably. My symbol of co-laboring does not rest necessarily on the editorial process itself—strenuous as it was. I would
have to say that some of our best times together occurred when
labor mellowed into leisure and we women, together with the bishops, would enjoy a meal together, reflect on weighty issues over
pizza and beer, and dream together of a church in which, to cite the
third goal articulated in *From Words to Deeds*, we "promote collaboration between men and women in the church" (§8). All I can say
is that one never forgets what it feels like when "mature Christians
express their unity in Christ and work together to accomplish his
mission in the world" (§9).

Dialogue at the highest level of civility takes place in the context
of spiritual friendship, which includes a commitment to personal
and shared prayer and an attentive listening to the divine directives
disclosed by the Holy Spirit. Spiritual friendship is a gift that has
been passed on to us by the Lord himself. As we read in the Gospel
of John, "No one has greater love than this, to lay down one's life
for one's friends. You are my friends if you do what I command
you. . . . I have called you friends, because I have told you everything I have heard from my Father" (John 15:13–15). This text suggests that soul-friends make sacrifices for one another. They obey
the laws of the Lord governing everything from adoration to sexual abstinence to fidelity in marriage. They respect the sacramen-
tality of human sexuality, refusing to reduce the beauty of the body
to mere genitality. Married persons uphold the goodness of unitive
and procreative love; single persons uphold the goodness of
celibacy for the sake of witnessing to what awaits us in eternity. All
respond to and uphold the authority of holiness. Each respects the
other at a level of heart-to-heart intimacy that unites us to God.

In his masterpiece on *Spiritual Friendship*, St. Aelred of Rievaulx
(1110–1167), a Cistercian abbot, models his thinking on the Oneness in Three shared by the Persons of the Blessed Trinity. He
reflects on the attraction, intention, and fruition of love. He sees
human friendship as a great good rooted in a person-to-Person

love relationship with Jesus. Of this grace of spiritual friendship, he writes:

> Was it not a foretaste of blessedness thus to love and thus to be loved; thus to help and thus to be helped; and in this way from the sweetness of fraternal charity to wing one's flight aloft to that more sublime splendor of divine love, and by the ladder of charity now to mount to the embrace of Christ himself; and again to descend to the love of neighbor, there pleasantly to rest?

Unlike some authors who cautioned against exclusive or particular friendships in community, Aelred viewed the inclusive style of spiritual friendship as the fruit of charity. It was a Christian virtue modeling the forming and interforming event of trinitarian love. Scripture teaches us that "God is love" (1 John 4:8). Aelred interprets this to mean also that "God is friendship," and that one "who dwells in friendship dwells in God." Lacking this gift, one risks being entirely alone.

Given this emphasis on loving one another as God has loved us, Aelred preached and practiced the Benedictine ideal that the monastic community, like the church, must be a school of love, where friendship with Christ flows over into befriending one another. Whereas pseudo-friendship in both single life and marriage has about it a carnal and possessive element, true friendship is rooted in the purity of Christ's love for his disciples, in the "mystical kiss" that seals our relationship with one another and with God. This self-giving disposition is the cement that holds a community together. It models for us on earth the communion of the saints in heaven. According to the *Catechism of the Catholic Church*, "whether it develops between persons of the same or opposite sex, friendship [lived chastely] represents a great good for all. It leads to spiritual communion" (2347). Faith in the Lord and commitment to his will are the basis of every soul-friendship. This alliance of oneness in God makes it possible for us to share prayer, to confess our secret hopes and dreams, to endure hardships and celebrate joys. It enables us not only to befriend one another but to offer inclusive love to all who come our way.

Just as the Father wills our total good, so do we will the entire good of the friends he sends to us. Our way with them is neither seductive nor manipulative; rather ours is an affinity rooted in appreciation and compassion. St. Aelred of Rievaulx rightly warns against an exclusivity that binds people together emotionally but at the expense of eroding their charity. He saw frankness and not flattery, generosity and not gain, patience in correction and constancy in affection as the marks of true friendship. In his opinion there is nothing more advantageous to seek in human affairs than friendship since, from being a friend to others, we become friends of God.

St. John of the Cross cautions souls under his direction to foster equal love (inclusivity) and equal forgetfulness (detachment). Lacking this capacity for befriending others, we may be caught in the barbed wire of resentment, envy, and jealousy. Equal love, as St. Paul teaches in 1 Corinthians 13:4–13, is patient and kind; it is never boastful or conceited, rude or selfish, and it does not come to an end as fickle romantic love is wont to do. Where there is strife, soul-friends seek avenues of reconciliation. When tempers flare and impatience prevails, they ask God for the grace to make a new start.

St. Teresa of Avila counsels her sisters in *The Way of Perfection* on the dangers that particular friendship or exclusivity poses. Instead of showing concern for the wounded condition in which all live since the Fall, one allows gossip and rash judgments to destroy community life. The saint asks her sisters to befriend one another by commending to God anyone who is at fault and striving to practice the virtue that is the opposite of the vice they observe.

Detached yet committed loving can be found when we open our hearts and souls to the all-inclusive love of Christ. Conflicts may arise that can pose a danger to compassion and peace, but with Christ standing between us we may find a way to face what is wrong and to work toward more respectful, life-giving relationships. It is often in times of crisis that friends discover their shared vulnerability and their need to care for one another as God cares for them. What better time could there be than this one of transition to the third millennium to draw women and men to the common ground of forgiveness and reconciliation at the foot of the cross, to reception of the Eucharist, to the celebration of the liturgy—not in opposition or anger but in partnership for the sake of promulgating the pastoral mission of the church.

The common ground that exists between us is Christ, who is the same yesterday, today, and tomorrow (Heb. 13:8). It was, after all, out of his single-hearted love for the Father that he embraced the community of disciples and set the church on the path of unity and diversity it must pursue in the coming era. The different perspectives we bring to this task—including our willingness to disagree agreeably—reveal our uniqueness and remind us of these lovely lines from Gerard Manley Hopkins's poem "As Kingfishers Catch Fire." For Hopkins the goal of life itself was to be conformed to the charity of Christ, who "plays in ten thousand places / lovely in limbs, and lovely in eyes not his / to the Father through the features of men's [and women's] faces."

Granted the need for both singularity and solidarity, I would like to applaud once more the immense contribution of single women and consecrated virgins to the church of old and of today. Though this vocation risks being marginalized and misunderstood it grants one committed to it a freedom for ministry and a sense of service to others that results not only in the grace of discipleship but also in the gift of spiritual parenting, a gift spectacularly used by Christ for the work of evangelization in women as historically diverse as Catherine of Siena and Dorothy Day, women who belonged, as we do, to the common priesthood of the people of God.

In fact, in *Strengthening the Bonds of Peace* (§9), it is said in unambiguous terms: "Pastors have a duty to welcome and provide for women's active participation in the [church's] life and mission as members of the common priesthood." The diversity of their gifts and the gifts of all women "should not be feared but recognized as a sign of the Church's vitality" (*From Words to Deeds* 5).

That these gifts have not always been affirmed is everyone's loss. That pastors are open to foster them will be to everyone's gain.

As we read in *From Words to Deeds*: "Ecclesial communion is characterized by a diversity of vocations and states of life, of roles, ministries, and gifts. Lay Christians have a duty as good stewards to offer these gifts to the church, while pastors have a reciprocal duty to foster them" (§9). In the history of spirituality, where would we be had Catherine of Siena not defied her mother's insistence that she marry by cutting off her golden hair? Many centuries later how would catechesis have been offered to the Indians of Quebec had not the widowed Blessed Marie of the Incarnation, with the permission of her young son who himself later became a religious, joined the Ursuline community that she wanted to enter before obeying her parents' insistence that she be married? In both instances, the gifts of these women were not respected. Vocations were imposed upon them that were not their choice, but, thanks to the guidance of grace and the empowerment they received from the Holy Spirit, their mission in the church bore lasting fruit.

Therefore, the first effect of collaboration between women and men, which for the church "is not an option" (*From Words to Deeds* 9), is a deepening *communio*, a rewarding reciprocity, a way to witness to the world that mature Christians must live in fidelity to their unique call while at the same time expressing their unity in Christ. As it states in Goal 3 of *From Words to Deeds*, "For the church, collaboration is not an option; it is the way that mature Christians express their unity in Christ and work together to accomplish this mission in the world."

What better examples of collaboration for the sake of accomplishing Christ's mission in the world do we need than that offered throughout our history by such spiritual friends as Francis and Clare of Assisi, Catherine of Siena and Blessed Raymond of Capua, Teresa of Avila and John of the Cross, Vincent de Paul and Louise de Marillac, Francis de Sales and Jane de Chantal, Thérèse of Lisieux and Maurice Belliere, Dorothy Day and Peter Maurin. Monica, the mother of Augustine, or married saints like Thomas

More, who would be God's servant before the king's, widowed saints like Blessed Marie of the Incarnation and Elizabeth Ann Seton, unnamed and unknown saints like our mothers and grandmothers, are bright lights on the long road to collaboration that ought to characterize the church of the third millennium. These partners in the mystery of redemption offer testimony to the depth and beauty of conformity to Christ for the sake of being his epiphany on earth. Consider these words penned by Thérèse of Lisieux to her spiritual friend, Brother Maurice, on April 25, 1897:

> You tell me, my Brother, to request the grace of martyrdom for you. I have often asked that grace for myself, but I am not worthy of it, and one can truly say with St. Paul: "It is not the accomplishment of the one who wills nor of the one who runs, but of God who has mercy."
>
> Since the Lord seems to want to give me only the martyrdom of love, I hope he will allow me through you to gain the other palm which we both desire. I notice with pleasure that the good God has given us the same attractions, the same desires. I have made you smile, my dear little Brother, by writing a poem called "My Arms." All right! I'm going to make you smile again by telling you that in my childhood I dreamed of fighting on battlefields. When I was starting to learn the history of France, the story of Joan of Arc's exploits delighted me. I used to feel in my heart the desire and the courage to imitate her. It seemed to me that the Lord destined me too for great things. I was not mistaken. But instead of voices from Heaven calling me to combat, I heard in the depths of my soul a voice that was gentler and stronger still: the voice of the Spouse of virgins was calling me to other exploits and more glorious conquests, and in the solitude of Carmel I understood my mission was not to crown a mortal king but to make the King of Heaven loved, to conquer for him the kingdom of hearts. (Patrick Ahern, *Maurice and Thérèse: The Story of a Love* [New York: Doubleday, 1998], 105-6).

Nothing would have come of the mutual ideals of Thérèse and Maurice for the church were it not for the intensity of their individual and common life of prayer. They remind us amidst the busiest of days to take time for reflection, time to listen alone and together to the Spirit of Love we all rely upon. They discovered that they could accomplish more together than if they stood alone. Each admired the light of holiness in the other. They became more holy through their knowledge of Christ in one another. Conflict, competition, excessive control, dismissive labeling, hostile takeovers, and lack of trust were simply not allowed to enter into the commitment these singular women and men made to Father, Son, and Holy Spirit. Thus, though they might have and often did feel alone, their letters and other exchanges reveal that they were never lonely.

May I close these reflections by citing again a paragraph from the first draft of the pastoral response to women's concerns for church and society titled, appropriately enough "Called to Partnership." To me these words, penned in 1988 (§§235–236) address the same concerns that draw us together today. They reflect that a wholesome formative spirituality flows from, and is not hampered by, our faith tradition because:

> To be faithful to our heritage scripturally and doctrinally means to respect the dignity of each human person, male and female. To follow Jesus means to be committed to living out just relationships in the Church and in the world. To become the kind of church God invites us to be means to work in solidarity with the poor, the rich, the sinners, with persons of distinction.

The mystery of partnership in the church is manifest in our baptismal call to faith and holiness as part of the little flock of Christ (see Luke 12:32). To live in Christ is the invitation all receive (see Gal. 3:28); to belong to Christ is the central reality in life (see Phil. 3:7–14); to refuse this vocation as coming from God is the most obstinate sin (see Gal. 3). The call to partnership in the church is thus fundamental to our entire heritage. We believe, therefore, that the cooperative mutuality of women and men by virtue of their baptism will more and more become a reality as our understanding of the grace and benefits of partnership grows. Only then can we be freed from the attitudes of fear, anger, and violence that divide and destroy the Christian community where all are challenged to abide in love (1 John 7:12).

## References

Aelred of Rievaulx. *Spiritual Friendship*. Translated by Mary Eugenia Laker. Washington, D.C.: Cistercian Publications, 1974.

Catherine of Siena. *The Dialogue*. Translated by Suzanne Noffke, O.P. Classics of Western Spirituality. New York: Paulist Press, 1980.

*The Collected Works of St. John of the Cross*. Translated by Kieran Kavanaugh, O.C.D., and Otilio Rodriguez, O.C.D. Washington, D.C.: ICS Publications, 1991.

Francis and Clare of Assisi. *The Collected Works*. Translated by Regis J. Armstrong and Ignatius C. Brady. Classics of Western Spirituality. New York: Paulist Press, 1982.

Francis de Sales and Jane de Chantal. *Letters of Spiritual Direction*. Translated by Péronne Marie Thibert. Classics of Western Spirituality. New York: Paulist, 1988.

Muto, Susan. *Celebrating the Single Life: A Spirituality for Single Persons in Today's World*. Bombay, India: St. Paul's, 1995.

Muto, Susan, and Adrian van Kaam. *The Woman's Guide to the Catechism of the Catholic Church*. Ann Arbor, Mich.: Servant, 1997.

*Partners in the Mystery of Redemption: A Pastoral Response to Women's Concerns for Church and Society*. Office of Publishing and Promotion Services. United States Catholic Conference. Washington, D.C. Publication No. 208-X.

Teresa of Avila. *The Way of Perfection*. In *The Collected Works*, vol. 2. Translated by Kieran Kavanaugh and Otilio Rodriguez. Washington, D.C.: ICS Publications, 1980.

Vincent de Paul and Louise de Marillac. *Rules, Conferences, and Writings*. Edited by Frances Ryan and John Rybolt. Classics of Western Spirituality. New York: Paulist Press, 1995.

# 2

## *Feminist Women's Spirituality:*

### *Breaking New Ground in the Church*

#### MIRIAM THERESE WINTER

M Y VISION OF THE CHURCH in the twenty-first century is one that is shared by a growing number of American Catholic women, and it is decisively, radically feminist. It promotes an understanding of liturgical worship and spirituality that has been honed by this perspective.

To be radical means to be rooted, deeply rooted, in the spirit of the living God, in the spirit of Jesus, and in the spirit of the biblical traditions that are recorded in the Scriptures and often hidden behind the texts. To be feminist, for me and for many others, means to be fully committed to the liberation of all peoples—women, children, and men, whether single, married, or in relationship with another, from every culture, class, race, religion, every possible situation. It means to be in the struggle for women's full participation in deciding the future of both religion and society, and that means the unequivocal inclusion of women in all decision-making and celebrational roles in the Roman Catholic Church. The wonderful women of the Bible, whose courageous witness to faith in the past lives on in women today, and the legacy of women throughout history confirm that the church is a phenomenon of the Spirit and, as such, is continually evolving. It is in this context that I speak to the theme of women, worship, and spirituality in our collective search for common ground.

Feminist spirituality, an aspect of women's spirituality, is a twentieth-century phenomenon that emerged within but is not limited to the United States. In the late 1960s, women began coming together in small groups for support and encouragement, and in those circles of relationship, they began to tell their stories. In telling their stories—in telling our stories—stories of pain and a passion for possibilities, stories of unfulfilled dreams and a vision for the future, we discovered we are not alone. Our individual stories resonated with the stories of countless women, for deep within our singular stories lies a thread that weaves us all together in a rich inner-connectedness. It is a web we would come to know and cherish as women's reality, an indestructible tie that binds, proclaiming that we are one.

As we told our stories, we were, in Nelle Morton's words, literally heard into speech. We found our voice, and we found in speaking through that voice that we had something to say. Moreover, when we said what we had to say, someone actually listened. Someone out there heard us and took us seriously, and that was exhilarating. From the listening and the speaking and the sharing emerged a new discovery, our own identity. We are not the labels we have inherited through our histories and our traditions. We are who we are, who we say we are. Now that was truly radical. We not only discovered our own identity, but we also found, many of us, the God for whom we had been searching, the God whom we had experienced, certainly, as we were growing up Catholic, but now were encountering in a new and far more personal way. God was no longer a God out there, but a God right here within us, a God we would know and name as very close, very concerned, very supportive of our own becoming. In this emerging awareness, then, we began to celebrate together our growth and our liberation.

Feminist women's spirituality cannot be disconnected from feminist worship. Whether we call it ritual, or liturgy, or worship, feminist women celebrate. It is integral to who we are as feminists and as women. We gather to celebrate in prayer and praise the God who is our God and the God of our Tradition—the larger Tradition, our Catholic Tradition, as well as the multiple women's traditions that have been recovered from the past and that are even now coming to birth in ourselves and in others. These celebrations have characteristics that differ from our traditional liturgical experiences. They are participational and relational, both in style and in substance.

When women meet, we tend to gather in a circle, where both power and leadership are shared. We listen to each other, face to face. We discern what another is trying to say, then respond in our own words, fully present and fully attentive, speaking from the heart. Such circular celebrations go deep, and they are carried out in a relational and embodied way. We don't just sit there. We lift our hands and our voices, we sing our songs and often dance, aware of being connected, contextually, to all other aspects of our lives and to the situations of life around us in the social-political and theological realms. Feminist spirituality, and therefore feminist ritual, means being linked to issues of birth and need and oppression and seeing them as intricately intertwined. Both are rooted in women's experience. Authentic feminist worship cannot be separated from issues of justice, not only individual justice concerns, but also the larger systemic and collective justice issues.

At the heart of feminist women's spirituality is telling it like it is. What began to emerge from our coming together were images and a language fully inclusive of women's experience and more reflective of our relationship to God. We were no longer hidden beneath patriarchal overlays, a subset of the sons of God the Father. We saw ourselves as daughters of Mother God and realized we are all sisters. We found ourselves with a language, with words that put us fully in the picture, not way out there at the margins, and we felt ourselves coming closer to the center of life and church and liturgy. As we explored themes of birthing and nurture, themes of life and of dedication, we were reborn and we were nurtured, and we felt fully alive again. The intricacies of women's experience and women's reality shaped our prayer and praise.

We discovered new images of God, and we did not have to look far to find them. We gazed deeply into our own experience and into biblical experience, which is actually peoples' experience recorded in the Bible. We saw in Scripture names and images that had been there all along and had simply been ignored. We began to sing and pray to God Sophia—which, by the way, really is in the Bible—to Sophia and Shekinah and Shaddai, biblical images and names for God. We sang songs, wrote prayers, and created liturgical rituals that named God in this way and in many other ways that brought God close to us and brought us close to God. By calling on God in womanly ways, we were able to see ourselves as Scripture has always seen us. In Genesis 1:27 we read that God created humanity in God's image, created female and male, created women as well as men in the image of the living God. We women image God. Don't let anyone tell you differently, because that would not be true. Biblical truth is this: we women are created in the image of God and we carry that image within us as a precious treasure. It is our legacy and our responsibility to reflect that image of God. Therefore, it is quite appropriate to want to shout from the mountaintops, or sing out in the assembly:

> *(All sing):*
>
> Rock-a my soul in the bosom of She Who Is.
> Rock-a my soul in the bosom of She Who Is.
> Rock-a my soul in the bosom of She Who Is.
> Oh, rock-a my soul.
>
> Oh, I know I come from Her.
> Oh, I know I go to Her.
> Oh, I know I live in Her.
> Holy is She who is God.
>
> Rock-a my soul in the bosom of She Who Is.
> Rock-a my soul in the bosom of She Who Is.
> Rock-a my soul in the bosom of She Who Is.
> Oh, rock-a my soul.[1]

Have you ever asked yourself how it happened that Abraham ended up with the bosom? I mean, really! Beth Johnson, thank you for the wonderful image of She Who Is, not only for lifting it up, but for making it theologically grounded.

Larger collectives emerged from our smaller, more intimate gatherings. A feminist style of leadership and a feminist experience of church community took root and flourished. There was genuine *koinōnia*, a group with bonds beyond the ordinary and boundaries that were permeable. There were no membership criteria, aside from being female. No one stopped you at the door to ask if you were Catholic—or, for that matter, even Christian—and there was nothing to prevent your full participation. You usually came bringing something—a flower, some cookies, your story, your pain, your joy, a piece of Good News, just as in 1 Corinthians 14, which says in its description of community worship that when they came together, each one brought something. Someone had a hymn, another a revelation. Others brought other things, whatever would contribute to shared praise and inspiration. It was in that spirit that women continued to gather and celebrate.

It was liberating. It is liberating, and because it is, it is also life-giving. This phenomenon of feminist spirituality and the dynamic of feminist liturgies have begun to shift the landscape of the institutional church. Within the patriarchal framework that defines our sacramental life is a vibrant women's reality with its multiplicity of perspectives shaped by race, culture, and the diversity of our own experience. At the heart of our Tradition now are a vast number of transformative traditions rooted in earlier traditions long lost and therefore invisible. These, together with other initiatives inclusive of both women and men, have led to a fundamental shift in our understanding of church. The church of the twenty-first century has been and is still being redefined, not necessarily as something totally new, but as something very ancient: a somewhat chaotic yet Spirit-led movement reclaiming that which has always been present and claiming it to the full. We know now in a much more experiential way that the church is not something to which we belong or someplace to go on occasion, but in essence, who we are. The church of the twenty-first century, like the church of the very first century, is multifaceted. Yes, we are the church, and while church is manifested in parishes already well established, church also exists where two or more gather to celebrate the presence of Jesus the Christ, who is there in spirit. Expressions of women-church are, we might say, like a parallel universe within American Catholic church communities and beyond.

Feminist women's spirituality has also had an impact on our understanding of authority. It reminds us time and again that, in addition to the perspective of the magisterium in canonical directives and official declarations, there is the larger authority of God's own Holy Spirit, which is far more elusive. Truly I say unto you, says Scripture: God's Spirit blows where God's Spirit wills. We cannot contain the Spirit, nor tell God what to do.

Scripture tells us that each one of us is a vessel of God's Holy Spirit. Women and men—all of us—are sanctuaries of that Spirit. The Spirit of God is within us. Believe it! And if we really believed it, we would have to take seriously those intuitions and insights that arise, because not to pay attention to them is to disregard God's Spirit. We may make mistakes, we feminists who believe in and celebrate and love feminist spirituality. We may make mistakes, but we believe that on this path there is a deep residue of truth, that we are moving beyond our boundaries in and through the Spirit. We know not quite where it will lead; therefore we do not know how to get to wherever we are to go. Nor do we know how we will become whoever it is we are called to be. But we do know that throughout the world there are many women on similar paths responding to the call of the Spirit. This is not so we can have a church of our own in which to celebrate by ourselves. It is so we can recover through a creative, intuitive, imaginative, instinctive reinterpretation of tradition new ways of being and behaving as Catholics, in order to live the fullness of what our Catholic tradition is. This cannot happen until we give statement to some of the things that have been dormant or silenced because they seemed too dangerous, too suspicious, too threatening to what has always been considered normative for all.

This is not a movement for women only but a vision for the church. There are feminist men who espouse feminist spirituality and their numbers are increasing. Like us, they are making a distinction between religion and spirituality, between religion that is outside of us, calling us to conformity, and a more intimate spirituality shaping us from within. Spirituality can be, and very often is, right there within religion, but it is not coterminus with it. It is a segregated world for some. Growing numbers of women are saying, God is speaking to me and saying this, and religion is saying that. The result is a disconnect that is personally crucifying. Feminist women's spirituality is categorically rejected, even though Catholicism embraces a variety of spiritual disciplines and there is precedent for following the path that is spiritually right for us. Those forms of traditional spirituality that have a lengthy history and institutional approval as the only acceptable way are not always right for women. Alternatives exist, however, paths validated by the Spirit: spontaneous, serendipitous, sensitive to women, not prone to categorization. These forms, reflective of a newly emerging spirituality, will guarantee into the future that our faith will have female children and that their children will learn about faith.

There is a possibility for ancient and new to coexist together with integrity, but you and I know, painfully and profoundly, how difficult it is to get a hearing for the things that matter most to us, and what a struggle it is to move initiatives of the Spirit from the margins to the center of institutional legitimacy. The process begins with simple strategies, but we are already tired of asking for such fundamental things as inclusive language. We women are not men, and our images of God are not exclusively male and never will be again, no matter how much those in positions of authority try to talk us into it. That doesn't work anymore. We should be beyond such issues by now as a new millennium unfolds around us, because there are far more critical concerns crying out to us to be heard.

The primary point is, in the end, we are all children of God, and therefore we are one. At the heart of feminist spirituality is the conviction that this is the gospel truth. Polarization comes when we refuse to accept God's unconditional love for all of God's creation. Characteristic of God's creation is unlimited diversity. Diversity is not just the color of one's skin or a multiplicity of cultures, but extends to include the distinctions among those of us who look a lot alike on the surface but differ deep within. More and more people are asking, "Is there room in this church for all of us?" Our children, who are the future of the church and who are becoming more and more disenchanted, ask: "Is there room in this church for me?"

The progress we have made as women in the church, gaining both visibility and voice, is our legacy to our children. We have some visibility now, but it is no longer enough for us just to be seen and not heard. We have found our voice, silent for so long, and we intend to use it. Among our goals are full inclusion in decision-making roles and in celebrational roles within institutional religion. Underlying these goals are the fundamental principles of justice and equality, for women as well as men.

In the 1990s I co-authored a national study assessing the potential impact of feminist women on institutionalized religion in the United States, published under the title *Defecting in Place: Women Claiming Responsibility for Their Own Spiritual Lives.* One of the chapters reports how American Catholic women feel about being Catholic. An overwhelming majority are presently "defecting in place," meaning, remaining within the tradition, not as they were but as they are. Previously, women with feminist inclinations who were frustrated with the Catholic Church might have gone to another denomination or simply walked away. Today, many are remaining in place with the hope of effecting change. We are staying right where we are, these women say, because this is our church, this is our tradition. This church, for all of its lack of understanding, is after all our home. It is where our roots are planted, where God is calling us to be.

To put it succinctly, what women really long for is a just church, not just a church. We want a living liturgy, not just a reenactment of a designated rite. When I say a living liturgy, I mean more than a liturgy that is alive. I mean a paradigm shift in perspective. We need to comprehend that God's word cannot be bound by a book or by rules and regulations, but is revealed primarily in life, in and through you and me. We are the word, you and I. In the Spirit of Word-made-flesh, we are God's Word enfleshed, every one of us. To be just, loving, patient, liberating, inclusive, hospitable, fair— we see that as our liturgy of the Word lived out in our lives. We want a living liturgy, not just a rite. We want a truly catholic church, one universally open to the Spirit, less vindictive, not so narrow. We must all work together to shape a church inclusive of all sorts of people, even radical feminists. In time we may discover that those who seem diametrically opposed to us are really not so bad after all, once we get to know each other for who we really are.

## NOTES

1. "Rock-a My Soul," by M.T. Winter © Medical Mission Sisters 1994 is recorded on the album *SpiritSong* and published in *Songlines*.

# Part 2

## Embodiment:

## Women and Men, Equal or Complementary?

O NE BEDROCK ISSUE on which the role of women stands or falls is theological anthropology, or the interpretation of what it means to be a human person before God through Christ in the power of the Spirit. Now that church teaching declares explicitly that women and men are created in the image and likeness of God, together and equally, the bone of contention has become how to interpret the bodily difference between males and females. The first round of debate has engaged two theories, an egalitarian anthropology of partnership and an anthropology of complementarity. The first emphasizes equality; the second accentuates difference. While these are theories, they have definite consequences in the social and political order. Both affirm the equality of women and men as *imago Dei*. Conflict arises, however, over whether and in what way sexual differences of the body should play out in social roles, with egalitarian anthropology declaring that people should be able to do whatever their giftedness equips them to do, and complementarity anthropology asserting that there are pre-given roles based on the difference that sexual identity makes. For the former, gender as a construal of sex is a social construction that can change with new experiences of history. For the latter, gender is such a "given" that a woman seeking a role traditionally reserved to men is said to be acting against her own nature.

To put the question sharply: Is the idea of women's "special nature" something revealed by God through the compassionate, liberating ministry of Jesus? Or is this idea an example (however unintentional) of discrimination on the basis of sex and thus contrary to God's intent?

Both papers delivered on this subject went creatively beyond the usual parameters of their respective theories. Using papal sources, Sara Butler crafted a fresh theology of complementarity that honors women and men in relation to each other. Due to an unexpected case of pneumonia, Elizabeth Johnson was not able to be present to speak for the egalitarian position; her paper is included here as part of the conversation. In a splendid and generous act of last-minute participation, Colleen Griffith stepped in with a genuinely new approach. She framed the egalitarian position in the fleshy context of the natural world, finding in the very fact of everyone's embodiment a source of unity more than division. Common ground emerges in a ringing endorsement of women's dignity while the question of social roles remains unresolved.

Their exchange sparked animated conversation. Some were pleased to hear a scholar putting forward Pope John Paul II's teaching so beautifully. A good many women expressed reservations about the primacy given to marriage and nuptial imagery in the theology of gender complementarity. Does this not limit what it means to be human to genital difference? Does this not leave many unmarried people out? Does it not ignore the diverse, nontraditional structure of the majority of American families? Does it not disallow loving relationships among same-sex couples? Some commented: "The reproductive function of human beings is exercised for a short time of a person's life and does not define the totality of a person. Women live more than half their life today without children. And brains are more important than genitals." Others were intrigued by the idea of bodily dignity as a concept that relates to social justice on many levels, for example, the environment and health care, along with its unitive function for egalitarian anthropology. Yet here too there are problems. Does not an overemphasis on equality lead to a corrosive focus on individualism? The question of social roles continued to arise. Why is there such a difference between what the pope says and women's experience in the church? If complementarity is linked with equality, why can trained women theologians not give a sermon during Mass? Searching for common ground, numerous participants tried to rename the terms of the debate in order to get beyond deadlock and express their own vision. An anthropology of mutuality or mutual interdependence won the prize.

— E. J.

# 3 ⎯⎯⎯⎯⎯⎯⎯⎯⎯⎯⎯⎯⎯⎯⎯⎯⎯⎯

## *Embodiment:*

## *Women and Men, Equal and Complementary*

### SARA BUTLER, M.S.B.T.

W E ARE HERE TO SEEK COMMON GROUND on issues that divide Catholics, in particular, Catholic women. The problem is identified in the title of this session: "Embodiment: Women and Men, Equal or Complementary?" The formulation of the topic reveals the conviction of many feminists that complementarity is irreconcilable with genuine equality. One has to choose between the two, therefore, and obviously equality wins! Others, myself included, maintain that there is no need to make a choice because both are true. Women and men are equal insofar as they are human persons, and complementary insofar as they are women and men. To put it another way: man and woman are equal in humanity, but not identical. On the one hand, they are of equal dignity or worth and possess equal rights as persons. On the other, male and female are two different bodily ways of being human, ordered to one another, that is, ordered to communion. In my opinion, the "either/or" formulation must give way to the typically Catholic "both/and": we are both equal and complementary.

## WHAT IS THE ISSUE?

Many Catholic feminists, without denying that human beings come in two sexes and that this has important consequences, feel compelled to reject the theory of complementarity. They charge that this theory implies an ordering that gives the advantage to men, and that it always "stacks the deck" against women—defining men as normative and superior and women as auxiliary and inferior. If it is shown that this patriarchal ordering is not implied, they object that complementarity nevertheless entails regarding woman and man as two halves of a whole, as if human character traits and social roles were divided down the middle—these to women, these to men—in a mutually exclusive way. They support their view by pointing to historical evidence that such a theory has been widely held and to present practice in the church, for example, the exclusion of women from the ministerial priesthood.[1]

According to Rosemary Radford Ruether, for example, "Any affirmation of difference means opposition and hierarchical relations of power and value." In her opinion, "we have no way of saying that men and women are different, and yet both are fully human, possess a fully human and equivalent nature, that neither is better or worse, normative or deficient."[2] Elizabeth Johnson appears to adopt the same analysis. She rejects complementarity because it represents for her "an unrelieved binary way of thinking," which "casts men and women as polar opposites, each bearing unique characteristics from which the other is excluded."[3] Many prominent Catholic feminists join Johnson in rejecting such a theory of complementarity.

I do not intend to defend a theory of sex complementarity that entails hierarchical relations of power and value or a "polar opposition" between the sexes. I too reject this view. I do not agree, however, that this is the only way to construe the complementarity of the sexes; it surely is not the theory the magisterium has been proposing for the past twenty-five years. The recent teaching of Pope John Paul II offers a theology of sex complementarity that does full justice, I maintain, to equality as well as difference.

But, to return to the formulation of the problem: Elizabeth Johnson suggests replacing the theory of complementarity (as she defines it) with a multipolar anthropological model. She wants to avoid the pitfalls of the "unisex" model, on the one hand, and to eliminate what she regards as an exaggerated focus on sexual difference, on the other. The anthropology she recommends features "one human nature celebrated in an interdependence of multiple differences."[4] In other words, she would include—along with sex—race, social condition, nationality, age, state of health, sexual preference, and cultural location as important differentiating factors ("anthropological constants") that shape a person's particular humanity and opportunity. According to her theory, sexual difference, while important,[5] has no real primacy in defining a person's identity.

What is in question, it seems to me, is the weight to be given to sexual difference in the definition of personal identity. What are the ontological meaning, the value, the ethical import, and the sacramental significance of sex? Some Catholic women, including Ruether and Johnson, think that because sexual difference is granted too much importance women suffer from stereotypes and are the subject of serious injustice, even (or especially) in the church. Other Catholic women disagree. We think that taking the personal meaning of sex seriously—for women and men both—is indispensable to the defense of the equal dignity of the sexes. This second position, of course, requires the elaboration of an alternative to the theory of sexual complementarity that both would regard as inadequate. I will draw on papal teaching[6] for such an alternative, not because nothing else is available,[7] but to put the feminist challenge in dialogue with it. There is no reason to beat a "dead horse" theory instead of taking serious account of what is actually being proposed!

CURRENT PAPAL TEACHING
ON THE COMPLEMENTARITY OF THE SEXES

The reconciliation of the two notions—the equality and the complementarity of the sexes—requires philosophical and theological

reasoning. It cannot be achieved by means of historical, physiolog-
ical, psychological, or political investigation. And whereas philosophical reflection is critically important, ultimately the nature of
humanity, created male and female in the image of God (Gen.
1:27), is fully illuminated only with the help of divine revelation.
In fact, the urgent need to defend the equality-in-difference of the
sexes has provoked significant discussions of trinitarian theology.[8]
We are created in the divine image not just as individuals but also
as persons-in-relationship who share an identical nature. Three
divine persons, one nature: you can surmise how the mystery of
the Trinity provides a model for the theoretical reconciliation of
equality and complementarity. This leads to my first point.

In the first place, the pope affirms the unity of human nature.
His theory of complementarity does not presume a "fractional"
division of human nature; that is, he does not hold that it takes two
halves—male and female—to make up a whole human being.[9]
Both man and woman possess the entirety of the human substance. Human nature is not "divided" or "shared" between the
sexes, but is possessed whole by each, though not in identical ways.
Consider the trinitarian analogy: the one divine nature is fully possessed by Father, Son, and Holy Spirit, but each divine Person pos-
sesses it differently. Just as the divine nature is not "parceled out"
to Father, Son, and Holy Spirit, so human nature is not parceled
out—one-half to men, the other half to women—but remains one,
unitary. Though possessed differently by the two sexes, there is one
identical nature. (This is not a "two-nature" theory!)

Second, the pope affirms the body. When we think of the fundamental constituents of human nature, we think of body and
soul. We are neither beasts nor angels, but embodied spirits.[10] The
faculties of the soul, intellect, and free will have long been identified as the distinctively human components that make us rational
animals. In the classical Christian explanation, these spiritual faculties constitute the divine image in our souls. We are capable of
knowing and loving God, and thus of fulfilling our vocation,
namely, communion with the triune God. In his phenomenologi-
cal analysis, the pope underlines the substantial unity of body and

soul in the human person. (This is not a "dualist" theory!) A person is a subject, he writes, "not only on the basis of his self-awareness and self-determination, but also on the basis of his own body."[11] Having a body belongs to "being human," belongs to our single human nature. We are not identical with our souls, as if we simply "inhabited" our bodies. We "are" our bodies. The body expresses the person. This is the case, logically, even apart from consideration of sexual difference.[12]

In the concrete, however, human nature exists only in one or the other sex, in women or in men. The third point, then, is that the two sexes are "two ways of being a body," two "incarnations" of human nature. The single human nature comes in a double issue: by reason of the body, every person is established as "he" or "she."[13] Sex, according to this theory, defines a personal mode of being in the world, not just a biological fact pertaining to male and female reproductive specializations.[14] Sexuality is more than "sex," more than the capacity for sexual intercourse as a bodily function. It belongs to the body-person, but also to the realm of personal relationships.

Fourth, man and woman are created for each other. They complement each other in a way that is mutual and reciprocal. They are partners, somewhat the way our two hands are. The right and left hands are made to work together; they "match" and are meant to exist in relation to each other. Woman and man are counterparts. This is neither a "two nature" theory nor a "unisex" theory, but a theology of complementarity which honors the biblical teaching that "God created humankind in his image . . . , male and female he created them" (Gen. 1:27). "Being a person in the image and likeness of God," writes the pope, "involves existing in a relationship."[15] This is a new move, and the pope makes it by regarding the body as a constitutive part of the divine image in humanity. In other words, the "double unity of male and female" reveals something about the divine trinitarian life, and vice versa. He teaches that man and woman are the image of God not only as individuals but together, in the communion of persons, the "one flesh" (Gen. 2:24) of married love.[16] The communion of love between

husband and wife mirrors the communion of love in the Blessed
Trinity. (Recall St. Augustine's beautiful trinitarian analogy: the
Lover, the Beloved, and their Love.) Husband, wife, and their marital covenant are an earthly reflection of this communion of love,
of this God who is Love (cf. 1 John 4:16). Papal teaching presents
this loving "communion of persons" as a relationship characterized by equality, mutuality, and reciprocity.[17]

This leads to the fifth point, the "nuptial meaning of the body."[18]
The pope's theology of complementarity takes embodiment very
seriously. The body expresses the person. Woman and man possess
human nature in two different bodily ways, ordered to each other,
that is, ordered to a communion of love. "To be human," the Holy
Father writes, "means to be called to interpersonal communion."[19]
The call to interpersonal communion is inscribed in our bodily
constitution as women and men. When the pope speaks of the
"nuptial" meaning of the body, he refers to the capacity for intimacy and self-donation which embodied persons have by reason
of their masculinity or femininity, and to their capacity to generate new life.

Sixth, any human community united in truth and love constitutes a certain image of the Holy Trinity, as *Gaudium et spes* (art.
24) teaches, but this is true in a special way of the community of
marriage. The primary expression of the complementary relation
between the sexes is found in marriage, where, by means of the
body, persons can make a "sincere gift of self" to one another that
fully expresses the meaning of sexual difference. Woman and man
exist not just side by side, but "for" each other.[20] Only a woman and
a man, as sexual counterparts, can be wife and husband to each
other; only they, together, can generate new life as the mother and
father of a child. These noninterchangeable sexual roles—husband–wife, father–mother—are personal, not merely biological,
and they are fundamental ways of fulfilling the vocation to love.
(These are not "stereotypes"!)

All this contributes to the conviction that sexual difference is
uniquely important. Sexual difference, according to this understanding, affects the human person much more intimately than
racial or ethnic differences, for it is ordered to the communion of

persons and the generation of children. Men and women from different racial and ethnic backgrounds, after all, are able to marry each other and have children. Racial and ethnic differences complement and enrich our society, but they do not structure the whole human community into families; they are not indispensable to the continuation of the species. Because sexual difference shapes one's capacity to love and give life, it has profound relevance for personal identity and for the social order.

Bodily sex is "a constituent part of the person" not just for the married but for everyone; it is part of one's concrete personal identity.[21] Young and mature single persons are not asexual; they love and give life in distinctively feminine and masculine ways, and by their chastity, they keep their dignity and self-respect. The same is true for women and men publicly consecrated to virginity or celibacy; they do not surrender their sexuality. In response to their vocation they make the complete gift of self to God and to others for his sake as embodied persons. In fact, a life dedicated exclusively to God and neighbor is a vivid sign of the ultimate vocation of every person.[22]

In sum, the pope offers a positive evaluation of sexual difference-in-equality and therefore finds it possible to identify and celebrate the specific gifts and contributions women and men make to the human community not only as individuals but also precisely as members of their respective sex. These distinctive gifts are not associated with one sex or the other in mutually exclusive ways, in his view, but are seen as characteristic feminine and masculine aptitudes or "styles" which enrich human coexistence in the family and in society. He observes, for example: "It is commonly thought that women are more capable than men of paying attention to another person."[23]

## Some Points of Clarification and Comparison

The theory, or theology, of complementarity that I am presenting, as I am sure you have noted, is drawn not from the empirical sciences or the concrete history of the "war between the sexes," but from the sources of revelation (e.g., the doctrine of the Trinity and a Christian rereading of Genesis).[24] It regards creation as male and female in the divine image as something positive. "And God saw that it was good" (Gen. 1:31).[25] Sexual difference is seen to be a value, an image of the Trinity in human persons oriented to communion, persons made for love. This is the very opposite of an anthropology that depicts the sexes as mutually antagonistic and competitive. This Christian anthropology explicitly affirms the equal personal dignity and rights of both women and men, and just as explicitly rejects the suggestion that one sex is superior to the other. It sees sexual difference as an invitation to communion, not to competition, and it finds a way to identify and celebrate the "genius" or original gifts of both sexes. According to this theology of sex complementarity, then, women do not have to conform to a male norm of behavior as the price of equality. Their "special prerogatives" can be respected and accommodated without injustice. This theory acknowledges that it is in our bodies that women are especially vulnerable to abuse, for example, and that it is as mothers that women have special needs.

The Christian anthropology I have just reviewed looks not only at the differences between persons as individuals (as the multipolar model does), but also, directly, at the difference between persons as women and men, at the difference between the sexes. It discovers the meaning of being male and female not by considering man and woman independently, standing side by side, but by considering them together, face-to-face, as made for each other. It considers the person not only as the subject of rights but also as the subject of relationships. And it is grounded not in the history of sin and oppression but in the history of redemption. In other words, this theory is governed by the Christian image of a God who is love, who freely creates out of love, and who invites our response of love. It is formally interested in discovering how relationships redeemed in Christ can repair and restore the damage done by sin, and lead to personal fulfillment.[26]

NOTES

1. In fact, this is not the fundamental reason for the church's judgment, but part of the theological reasoning advanced to illustrate its meaningfulness. See *Inter insigniores*, art. 5, §1.

2. "We Need Better Words Than Black and White," *National Catholic Reporter*, September 16, 1988, p. 15. In my opinion, "complementarity" is a way of saying just this, but it adds the idea that the sexes are ordered to one another.

3. Elizabeth Johnson, *She Who Is: The Mystery of God in Feminist Theological Discourse* (New York: Crossroad, 1992), 154–55.

4. Ibid., 155.

5. While she asserts its importance, Johnson fails to offer a positive explanation of the meaning, value, or symbolism of sexual difference.

6. This teaching may be found in the apostolic letter "On the Dignity and Vocation of Women" (*Mulieris dignitatem*, 1988), *The Theology of the Body* (Boston: Pauline Books & Media, 1997), and *Pope John Paul II on The Genius of Women* (Washington: USCC, 1997). For the points pertinent to this topic, see my essay "Personhood, Sexuality and Complementarity in the Teaching of Pope John Paul II," *Chicago Studies* 32 (April 1993): 43–53.

7. For authors who are in dialogue with the papal teaching, see Prudence Allen, Benedict Ashley, Donald Keefe, Francis Martin, Monica Migliorino Miller, Mary Aquin O'Neill, Mary Timothy Prokes, and Mary Rousseau.

8. For reconstructions inspired by feminist theological concerns, see Johnson, *She Who Is;* and Catherine Mowry LaCugna, *God for Us: The Trinity and Christian Life* (San Francisco: Harper, 1991).

9. For a critique of the "fractional" theory, see Prudence Allen, "Integral Sex Complementarity and the Theology of Communion," *Communio* 17 (Winter 1990): 523–44.

10. See Mary Rousseau's development of this idea in "The Ordination of Women: A Philosopher's Viewpoint," *The Way* 21 (July 1981): 211–24.

11. *Theology of the Body*, 40.

12. Ibid., 41–43.

13. Ibid., 42–45, 49.

14. This is an important point of difference from feminist anthro-

pologies, which often distinguish "sex" (the biological fact of being male or female) from "gender" (the socially constructed expectations of the sexes). Insofar as "sex" is regarded as prepersonal, it is hard to discover the specific value of virginity or motherhood.

15. "On the Dignity and Vocation of Women," art. 7.

16. *Theology of the Body,* 48–51.

17. See John S. Grabowski, "Mutual Submission and Trinitarian Self-Giving," *Angelicum* 74 (1997): 489–512.

18. Ibid., 63–66.

19. "On the Dignity and Vocation of Women," art. 7.

20. Ibid.

21. *Theology of the Body*, 49.

22. "On the Dignity and Vocation of Women," art. 20.

23. Ibid., art. 18. See *Pope John Paul II on The Genius of Women* for a further elaboration of this perspective.

24. Space does not permit reflection on the pope's use of the "great analogy," the mystery of the covenant between Christ and the church. See "On the Dignity and Vocation of Women," arts. 23–25. Empirical investigation, generally speaking, lends support to this theology.

25. See Donald J. Keefe, "The Sacrament of the Good Creation: Prolegomena to the Discussion of the Ordination of Women," *Faith & Reason* 9 (1983): 143–54.

26. Christian anthropology must be based on the vision of redeemed relationships. See "On the Dignity and Vocation of Women," arts. 9–10.

# 4

## Imaging God,
## Embodying Christ:

### Women as a Sign of the Times

#### Elizabeth A. Johnson

#### A New Voice

FOR SEVERAL THOUSAND YEARS, society ran on the idea that men by nature were fit to lead in the intellectual, political, and economic spheres. Women's main role was to bear children for the men and, in any way possible, to support them in their difficult endeavors. One regrettable result was women's silence and invisibility in the public realm. It is not the case that women were unimportant: their work as nurturers and formers of young children had a strong impact on society. Nor was it the case that women were not there in the midst of events, or did not speak, or did not even have influence behind the scenes. But, with a few outstanding exceptions, their work and their words were not considered worth recording because of their subordinate position.

This arrangement in society prevailed also in the church. It is a poignant loss that we have no record of the words of the women disciples of Jesus preaching his message, discussing among themselves what faith might mean, and contributing to the postresurrection decisions of the community—though traces of this activity can be found in the Scriptures. We have little knowledge of the faith experience, theological insight, and practical pastoral gifts of the millions of women who formed half of the church community in subsequent centuries—though their prayer, their quest for God, and their creative initiatives and goodness toward others irreplaceably built up the Christian tradition we have inherited. Instead, as one female biblical scholar wrote early on after conducting a reconnaissance of women's position:

> A masculine monopoly in religion begins when Miriam raises her indignant question, "Does the Lord speak only through Moses?" Since then, in all three of the great religious groups stemming from the land and books of Israel—Judaism, Christianity, and Islam— men have formulated doctrine and established systems of worship offering only meager opportunity for expression of the religious genius of womankind. . . . If a woman born and bred in any of these faiths takes a comprehensive look at the form of religion best known to her, she discovers that it is masculine in administration, in the phrasing of its doctrines, liturgies, and hymns. It is man-formulated, man-argued, man-directed.[1]

After millennia of this masculine monopoly in religion, technically called *patriarchy,* the rule of the father, women in our day around the globe are emerging into voice and visibility in both the private and public domains, even questioning whether these are appropriate divisions of reality. With varying degrees of success, they are demanding the rights and responsibilities befitting their dignity as human persons. In his encyclical *Pacem in Terris* (Peace on Earth) 1963, John XXIII took note of this new movement and named it, along with the rise of the poor working class and the emergence of new nations beyond colonialism, as one of the signs of the times that demand the attention of the church. Interpreted in a theological sense, signs of the times arise because God continues to speak and act in and through human history. The church therefore needs to look to the world to discover God's designs for the present time. History, in this view, ceases to be the place where the church simply applies binding principles that are derived from philosophical reasoning. Rather, "it becomes the place of on-going revelation."[2] Like the demand of the poor for economic justice and the right of African nations to self-governance, the rise of women's claims to human dignity stems from God's design for the world. In the words of this blessed pope:

> It is obvious to everyone that women are now taking a part in public life. This is happening more rapidly perhaps in nations with a Christian tradition, and more slowly but broadly among peoples who have inherited other traditions or cultures. Since women are becoming ever more conscious of their human dignity, they will not tolerate being treated as inanimate objects or mere instruments, but claim, both in domestic and in public life, the rights and duties that befit a human person.[3]

Since history is the place of ongoing revelation, naming the rise of women as a "sign of the times" locates this struggle on the side of the angels.

Pope John XXIII was discerning God's will in the history of the world outside the church, but inevitably the changing role of women in contemporary society is spilling over into the church, which after all is made up of contemporary women and men. Now the consciousness of women's dignity as equally created in the image of God and redeemed by the grace of Christ raises new issues about the standing and participation of women in the life of the community. They will not tolerate being treated as anything less than mature human persons in the community of Christ's disciples. Thanks to our culture's wealth and technology, at least some of these reflections and debates are being published. Women's silence is being broken. Their words are being transcribed. Future generations will have a way of hearing how some women of our era wrestled with the call of the ever-coming God of history.

Basic to any discussion of women's full humanity with its rights and duties is the church's teaching about the identity of human beings before God: human persons are created by God in God's own image and likeness; they are redeemed from sin by Christ, made holy by the Spirit, called to responsibility in and for this world, and destined for joyous life eternal in the embrace of God. There is great promise in this teaching as women claim its power to shape their own identity equally with that of men. The situation is not so simple, however. Along with these ringing affirmations about humanity in general, theology and ordinary doctrinal teaching have denied that they apply to women, or apply only partially. It is instructive to trace this ambiguity, to make clear what traditional knots have to be untied.

The first chapter of Genesis depicts what happens on the sixth day of creation: "Then God said, let us make humankind in our image, after our likeness; and let them have charge of the fish of the sea, the birds of the air, the cattle and all the earth, and every creeping thing that creeps upon the earth. So God created humankind in his own image; in the image of God he created them; male and female he created them. And God blessed them . . ." (Gen. 1:26–28a). This text makes a major claim: women and men together, equally, relationally, as human beings, are created in the image and likeness of God. Not one more than the other, not one over the other, but together as the human race.

The New Testament takes this teaching for granted and gives it a Christian twist in the light of baptism. Paul writes to the Galatians: "For as many of you as were baptized into Christ have put on Christ. There is no more Jew or Greek, slave or free, male and female, but you are all one in Christ Jesus" (Gal. 3:27–28). This text explicitly teaches that baptism clothes human beings with Christ equally, without distinction based on race (Jew or Greek), or economic and social class (slave or free), or gender (male and female). Biblical scholars note that Paul is quoting here an early Christian baptismal hymn, possibly sung as the newly baptized emerged from the water and were clothed in a white robe. Visually, all distinctions by which society organized itself were erased. A new principle based on participation in Christ now governs this community. The social ramifications of this spiritual transformation can be glimpsed in the Scriptures, where the social elites do not necessarily have precedence in the community: the first shall be last. The attractiveness of this principle to those on the underside is attested to by the criticism of the nascent Jesus movement as a religion of slaves and women.

The insight of these two biblical texts, along with many supportive texts, grounds the church's constant teaching that all
human beings, women and men alike, including all races and
classes, are created in God's image and likeness and redeemed by
Christ in the Spirit. Of this there can be no doubt.

## DENIED

We have inherited a tradition of theology, however, that has diminished this core teaching by privileging men over women as images
of God. This began to happen when early Christian theologians
expressed their ideas in the categories of Greek philosophy, so
influential in their culture. Classical Greek philosophy divided all
reality into two spheres: matter and spirit. Everything that exists
belongs to one sphere or the other. Greek thought also ranked
these two spheres, prizing spirit, which is the realm of light, the
eternal, the divine, over matter, which is the realm of darkness,
change, and death. When it came to human beings, this philosophy
identified men with spirit and women with matter. Thus men by
nature are nearer to the divine, endowed with soul, rationality,
power to take initiative, power to act, while women by nature are
oriented to the body, irrational and uncontrollable emotions, passivity, and receptivity. For their own good, women need to be subject to men, who can guide them toward the higher realm. This
dualistic vision results in a world where men are superior humans,
fit to rule in both public and private realms, while women exist
with an inferiority for which there is no remedy.

Taking this theory into theology set up a real and lasting ambiguity about whether women were truly created in the image of
God. Consider the following influential examples: Tertullian,
drawing on man's fear of being tempted by woman, infamously
interpreted Genesis 3 as a story of sexual temptation and cast all
women in the role of Eve:

> Do you not realize that you are each an Eve? The curse of God on
> this sex of yours lives on even in our times. Guilty, you must bear
> its hardships. You are the gateway of the devil; you desecrated the
> fatal tree; you first betrayed the law of God; you softened up with

your cajoling words the one against whom the devil could not pre-
vail by force. All too easily you destroyed the great image of God,
Adam. You are the one who deserved death, and because of you the
Son of God had to die.[4]

Augustine, while affirming that woman is equal to man in her soul,
denied the fullness of the image of God to woman because of her
body and her social role. He wrote:

> the woman with her husband is the image of God in such a way
> that the whole of that substance is one image, but when she is
> assigned her function of being a helper, which is her concern alone,
> she is not the image of God; whereas in what concerns the man
> alone he is the image of God as fully and completely as when the
> woman is joined to him in one whole [she needs the male head for
> rationality and control].[5]

Perhaps the most succinct expression of this denial of the image of
God to women is that of Thomas Aquinas. In the *Summa Theologiae* he defined woman as "a defective male," "a misbegotten male,"
because of the biological idea that if the sperm that was implanted
had developed perfectly, a son would be born (perfection begets
perfection); a daughter is the result of something going wrong
(*Summa Theologiae* I, q. 92, a. 1).

The denial of women's dignity as fully and equally created in the
image of God pervades the tradition. As with any prejudice, once
this gets put into place structurally, it begins to shape consciousness; after a while it is taken for granted. Over time women inter-
nalize the self-image that the oppressive system feeds them and
instinctively think of themselves as less than worthy. Not all
women do this—we have always had feisty women who refused
that definition. But it becomes a pervasive idea that affects all the
generations in some way.

REAFFIRMED

In our day, official Catholic teaching has vigorously restated the
core belief that women and men are equally made in God's own

image. The first major statement appeared in Vatican II's Pastoral Constitution on the Church in the Modern World (*Gaudium et spes*) in the context of affirming social justice for all peoples:

> Since all persons possess a rational soul and are created in God's likeness, since they have the same nature and origin, have been redeemed by Christ, and enjoy the same divine calling and destiny, the basic equality of all must receive increasingly greater recognition. True, all persons are not alike from the point of view of varying physical power and the diversity of intellectual and moral resources. Nevertheless, with respect to the fundamental rights of the person, every type of discrimination, whether social or cultural, whether based on sex, race, color, social condition, language, or religion, is to be overcome and eradicated as contrary to God's intent. For in truth it must be regretted that fundamental personal rights are not yet being universally honored. Such is the case of a woman who is denied the right and freedom to choose a husband, to embrace a state of life, or to acquire an education or cultural benefits equal to those recognized for men.[6]

Doctrinal teaching about the human race issues in social consequences whereby every person's dignity must be respected. Moreover, the denial of women's fundamental freedom to construe their lives becomes the illuminating example of what may go wrong for all the other groups. In traditional theological language, whatever is contrary to God's intent is a sin. This document asserts that discrimination against women on the basis of their sex is sinful.

In 1988 Pope John Paul II in his encyclical *Mulieris dignitatem* (On the Dignity and Vocation of Women) writes in an even more explicit way. "Both man and woman are human beings to an equal degree, both are created in God's image."[7] Again, a human being "is a person, man and woman equally so, since both were created in the image and likeness of the personal God." And again, the biblical text of Genesis "provides sufficient bases for recognizing the essential equality of man and woman from the point of view of their humanity. From the very beginning both are persons . . . the woman is another 'I' in a common humanity." And again, "both man and woman are like God. For every individual is made in the image of God." The whole letter is filled with this affirmation, which can now be found also in the *Catechism of the Catholic Church*. Clearly, the position that held women's human dignity to be less worthy than men's is being corrected in theory.

This shift has tremendous consequences for the church's social teaching insofar as it serves to promote the well-being of women in concrete physical, social, and spiritual ways. For all is not well with women in the world. According to United Nations statistics compiled at the turn of the millennium, women, who form half of the world's population, do three-fourths of the world's work (in hours), receive one-tenth of the world's monetary income, own one-hundredth of the world's land (99 percent of the earth is owned by men), form two-thirds of the world's illiterate adults, and together with their dependent children form three-fourths of the world's starving people. To make a bleak picture worse, women are raped, battered, prostituted, sold into sexual slavery, and murdered by men to a degree that is not reciprocal. Violence against the dignity of women made in the image of God is rampant on a global scale, including domestic violence. In light of this situation, which entails so much suffering, the importance of insisting on the *imago Dei* doctrine for women becomes clear. Its logic provides a strong basis for promoting social justice for women and the girl child.

## New Ambiguity: Women's Special Nature?

Many who read John Paul II's endorsement of women's equality with men as image of God wonder why it does not lead him to posit equality in all ministries of church life and governance. The reason is that he is still using the traditional dualistic view that men and women embody human nature in two contrasting ways, which means that they each possess special characteristics, which means that they must play distinct social roles. What makes the papal position an advance from previous thinkers who use the dualistic masculine-feminine framework is that he declares the two sides of the divide to be of equal value and mutually related.

Separate but equal and related becomes the essential principle of this anthropology.

There is real improvement here from the classical tradition, where women were vilified as temptresses and denied the dignity of being fully created in the image of God. Departing from centuries of church tradition, papal teaching now emphatically affirms the equality of women and men before God. The ambiguity arises, however, because the limits of the dualistic model, insofar as it posits essential differences between masculine and feminine versions of human nature, prevent this newly retrieved teaching on equality of nature from being applied to equality of social roles. "Masculine nature" with its active orientation to rationality, order, and decision making is equipped for leadership in the public realm. "Feminine nature" with its receptive orientation to love, life, and nurturing is fit for the private domain of childbearing, homemaking, and care for the vulnerable. It does not escape women's notice that the proposed division of labor inevitably privileges men in terms of social, political, and economic power. In the church this model justifies the practice of excluding women from positions of ritual leadership and public governance.

Keeping in mind how positively John Paul II assesses "feminine" human nature allows us to see the praise intended when he holds up Mary, the mother of the Redeemer, as the model whom all women should strive to emulate. As with Mary, women's true vocation is motherhood, whether physical or spiritual. Like Mary, women should develop certain characteristics that will enable them to live their true vocation to the utmost. In his encyclical *Redemptoris mater* (Mother of the Redeemer) he lists these virtues as follows:

> It can thus be said that women, by looking to Mary, find in her the secret of living their femininity with dignity and of achieving their own true advancement. In the light of Mary, the church sees in the face of women the reflection of a beauty which mirrors the loftiest sentiments of which the human heart is capable: the self-offering totality of love; the strength that is capable of bearing the greatest sorrows; limitless fidelity and tireless devotion to work; the ability

to combine penetrating intuition with words of support and encouragement.[8]

Whatever may be the praiseworthy value of this list of virtues, the fact that they are "feminine," applied to women but not to men, makes them suspect. They are the habits of the helper, the auxiliary, the handmaid, not that of the resister of oppression let alone the self-actualizing, creative leader. In situations of abuse, such sentiments can even be dangerous to life and limb. Assigning them to women in the private domain may challenge women to develop a spiritual life, but it also serves to deny them opportunities for equal partnership in society.

On balance, so-called papal feminism is a kind of romantic feminism. It holds women in such an idealized regard that they are judged to be too good to get involved in the messiness of the public realm. Many women respond as did one of my college students in a paper on "The Dignity and Vocation of Women": "As a young woman of the late twentieth century do I want to be so highly exalted? No, I would rather be equal." One young man in my class also had a fascinating insight: "Saying that women are more fitted to love means that they are better able to follow Jesus' teaching to love God and your neighbor with all your heart. Where does that leave me? Second best?" The point being, of course, that by boxing women's and men's identities into innate differences based on traditional gender stereotypes, a dualistic anthropology inevitably compromises the human and spiritual potential of both.

A number of women scholars have found this dualistic anthropology deficient, arguing that while the cells of women's and men's bodies are indeed different in terms of the sex chromosome (XX and XY), and while sexual differentiation is indeed irreplaceable for reproduction, and while deep mutuality between a woman and a man ranks as one of the most profound relationships on earth, nevertheless, the way these differences play out in the social sphere is historically conditioned. Family roles, educational opportunities, and social expectations shape character. Change these, and new possibilities emerge, as is indeed happening in society today. More liberating and truer to experience is a holistic egalitarian anthropology of partnership. In this line of thought a person's characteristics and vocation are not predetermined by sex, vital though this is as a component of personal identity. Rather, human aptitudes exist across a wide spectrum for women and men. Women can be rational and great at leadership; men can be loving and nurturing. And rational women and nurturing men can form beautiful mutual relationships. In fact, the range of differences among women themselves ends up being just as great or even greater than differences between some women and some men. Accordingly, social roles are not to be preassigned according to gender but engaged in according to persons' gifts, callings, and education.

Despite this ongoing dispute over anthropology, we should not lose sight of the central fact: the church is now teaching authoritatively that women are fully and equally created in the image of God.

## New Ambiguity:
## Women in the Image of Christ?

With the "image of God" dignity of women finally granted, at least in theory, a new field of dispute has opened regarding the "image of Christ." Women may be theomorphic, but are they capable of being christomorphic? When the Vatican document *Inter insignores* (1976) declared that women were not permitted to enter the ministerial priesthood, one of the reasons given was that since Christ was a man, meant not inclusively but in the gendered sense of the male sex, women, who were not men, could not act *in persona Christi* during the Eucharist. The sacrament needs to draw on a natural analogy, the argument goes, and so the priest has to look like Jesus in terms of his masculinity. As many commentators noted at the time, this is not a teaching drawn from tradition but a new idea crafted by the Vatican office.[9] Focused on Jesus' sex to the exclusion of his race, age, and other human characteristics, its logic reduces the theological identity of the believer as the image of Christ to physical similarity to the male body. Criticisms of this idea's erroneous theology have been so strong, and it has been shown to be so dangerous to the church's teaching on the meaning of baptism, that it has been quietly dropped from more recent official declarations on the subject. But the damage has been done, as people continue to repeat this simplistic idea.

In place of naive physicalism, Scripture and tradition teach that being the image of Christ means sharing in Christ's loving life through the power of the Spirit. This is a communal identity brought about through baptism. Dying and rising with Christ, being transformed by his grace and living now in the Spirit, the community participates in Christ's life so truly that it can be called the body of Christ. This community is called "to be conformed to the image" of Christ (Rom. 8:29). The Greek of this text is instructive, for the members of the community are identified as *sym-morphos* to the *eikōn*, that is, sharing the form of the likeness, or being formed according to the image of Christ. No distinction on the basis of sex is made, or needed; being christomorphic is not a sex-distinctive gift. Nor does it mean that women lose their femaleness or embodied sexuality. The image of Christ lies not in sexual similarity to the human man Jesus but in coherence with the narrative shape of his compassionate, liberating life in the world, through the power of the Spirit. Each member who lives the life of Christ is an icon of Christ in his or her whole enfleshed personal existence: "Don't you know that your bodies are members of Christ?" (1 Cor. 6:15). Theologically, the capacity of women and men to be *sym-morphos* to the *eikōn* of Christ is identical.

There is the further teaching of the Gospel that the image of Christ resides most really in poor and suffering people, those who are hungry and homeless, sick and in prison. The great judgment scene in Matthew resonates with the question, "Lord when did we see you in need this way?" In other words, where was your image that we might have recognized you? The answer is uncompromising and has evoked two thousand years of loving Christian action at its best: "As long as you did it to one of the least of these my brothers [and sisters], you did it to me" (25:40); and "As long as you did not do it to one of the least of these, you did not do it to me" (25:45). This parable of Jesus continues to challenge every tendency toward triumphalism or complacency in the church.

Being the image of Christ, then, does not entail being a xerox copy of Jesus' sexual self. Rather, it consists of sharing in the life of Christ's love of God and love of neighbor, following Jesus on the path of discipleship.

This fundamentally egalitarian truth is bedrock to the church's whole life and teaching. It grounds the baptismal liturgy, where both male and female persons receive the sacrament by the same ritual and words and to the same effect: "As many of you as were baptized into Christ have clothed yourselves with Christ" (Gal. 3:27). It permeates the funeral liturgy, celebrated with the same texts and rite whether the individual involved is woman or man, for the theological character of their being *in Christ* is identical. It lights up the martyrdom tradition. As Vatican II taught, the martyrs are assimilated (*assimilatur*) and configured (*conformatur*) to an especially intense image of Christ, for the martyr "perfects that image even to the shedding of blood"[10]—without distinction based on sex. This truth also undergirds the call to holiness in the church, for "all of us," as Paul wrote, "are being transformed into that same image [Christ's] from one degree of glory to another" (2 Cor. 3:18). And it pervades the doctrine of the saints, who, as Vatican II taught, shared our humanity and yet were transformed into especially successful "images of Christ," again without any sex-specific comparisons.[11]

The ambiguity of recent vintage regarding women's capacity to be images of Christ is truly unfortunate, for it has no basis in doctrine and in fact contradicts the central teaching of the church. Created women, baptized women, martyred women, sinful and redeemed women, holy women of all varieties: all are genuinely *imago Dei, imago Christi*. Anything less distorts God's good creation and shortchanges the theological truth of women's identity in Christ.

## THE CONVERSATION

This short reconnaissance of the church's teaching about human persons before God and the struggle to apply it fully to women makes clear that counting women in as genuine members of the human race and partners in the Christian community has been dicey and difficult. Today's efforts to grapple with this issue are fraught with significance, for the theory about who women are leads inevitably to practice. Women's claim to full membership in the human race and the church entails new forms of relationship between women and men encoded in structures, laws, and customs. The transformation involved is nothing short of seismic. And women themselves disagree about how best to negotiate the changes.

However, if the glory of God is the human being fully alive, as Irenaeus declared, then the tensions of the present moment are filled with hope. For resisting women's subordination and struggling for full recognition of women's dignity is clearly the work of the Spirit. And She will not be quenched. From this point on there can be no future for the church that women have not had a pivotal hand in shaping. And women are silent and invisible no longer.

## NOTES

1. Margaret Brackenbury Crook, *Women and Religion* (Boston: Beacon, 1964), 1, 5.

2. John XXIII, *Pacem in terris* (New York: America Press, 1963), §41.

3. Peter Henriot et al., *Catholic Social Teaching: Our Best Kept Secret* (Maryknoll, N.Y.: Orbis, 1988), 18.

4. Tertullian, *On the Dress of Women* 1.1 (CSEL 70.59); cited in Elizabeth Clark, *Women in the Early Church* (Collegeville, Minn.: Liturgical Press, 1983), 39.

5. Augustine, *The Trinity* 12.7.10, trans. Edmund Hill (Brooklyn, N.Y.: New City Press, 1991), 328; see Kim Power, "Woman, man, and the *imago Dei*," in her *Veiled Desire: Augustine on Women* (New York: Continuum, 1996), 131–57.

6. *Gaudium et spes,* the Pastoral Constitution on the Church in the Modern World §29, in Walter Abbott, ed., *The Documents of Vatican II* (New York: America Press, 1966).

7. John Paul II, *On the Dignity and Vocation of Women, Origins* 18:17 (October 6, 1988) §6. The next two quotations are also from §6; the last quotation is from §7.

8. John Paul II, *Mother of the Redeemer, Origins* 16:43 (April 9, 1987) §46.

9. Carroll Stuhlmueller, ed., *Women and Priesthood* (Collegeville, Minn.: Liturgical Press, 1978), 85-110.

10. *Lumen gentium,* the Dogmatic Constitution on the Church, §42, in Abbott, ed., *Documents of Vatican II.*

11. Ibid., §50.

# 5

## Human Bodiliness:

## Sameness as Starting Point

### COLLEEN M. GRIFFITH

T HE TITLE OF THIS GATHERING of the Common Ground Women's Symposium excites me. *"Embodiment"* has become a rich focus for theological reflection. Although historically Christian treatment of the body has been ambiguous, resulting in bodies being more feared than revered, recent theological interest in the body has fostered a celebration rather than a problematization of human bodily life. As individual persons and communities of faith catch fuller glimpses of the religious significance of human bodiliness, one begins to imagine a church less suspicious and fearful of the body, less prone to hierarchical ordering of bodies, and more eager to acknowledge bodiliness as the location of a Christian spirituality.

The subtitle of today's session leaves me feeling less enthusiastic. *"Women and Men: Equal or Complementary?"* suggests an exploration of embodiment from a standpoint of difference. What gets hidden from view by this starting point is our shared human bodiliness. Bodies are the inescapable fleshly facts of human existence. The opportunity to recognize our radical sameness and interconnection through the commonality of human bodiliness lessens when we begin our reflection on embodiment from the position of difference.

"Equality or complementarity?" is not a new question. It has resulted in some heated and deeply politicized debates. One wonders whether honest searching for the truth on this one has been replaced by a jockeying of opposing sides with definite agendas regarding the outcome. It is helpful to note the particular contexts in which the "equality versus complementarity" issue is raised and the positions of power of the persons raising it. I sense that there are many subtexts beneath this question.

Institutional powers of church and society have argued predominantly from the standpoint of complementarity. But is the result a life-enhancing transformation for women? There is not much evidence of this.

I understand the term "complementarity anthropology" to refer to a division of persons into two kinds, male and female, one that carries with it a designation of characteristics and qualities specific to each sex. Complementarity anthropology describes women as having a particular nature, God-ordained as such, that helps to identify characteristics that are feminine/womanly and roles that are more appropriately womanly than others. It has been said, for example, that women, by virtue of their distinct embodiment, are more passive, whereas men are more active. Women are thought to be more receptive, while men are viewed as driven. Women are said to focus inwardly, whereas men are seen as outward-bound; women are more relational, favoring connections, and men are more autonomous. Women are described as intuitive and emotional, whereas men are said to gravitate toward the rational. A bipolar picture of humankind comes into view.

I find claims for complementarity to be problematic and dangerous. My critique of the anthropological construct of complementarity is fourfold:

1. One underlying assumption of a complementarity anthropology is that there is something tangibly "male" and "female" that can be said of men and women respectively, *apart from social and historical circumstances.* Proponents of this construct define women and men in purely singular terms that exclude the diversity

and uniqueness of persons. Yet, if those of us assembled today were to make a list of the typical stereotypes found under the two headings "Male" and "Female," I suspect few of us would identify exclusively with the qualities listed under one of those headings only. What we might notice, however, is the number of human qualities listed under the "Female" column that are still more undervalued in church and society than their parallels in the "Male" column, and the need for a retrieval of these qualities on the part of both women and men.

2. A complementarity anthropology focuses narrowly on the genital organs of women and men, and the specific mechanics of heterosexual sexual experience. This privileges an important but limited dimension of bodily existence. Should the sexual characteristics of human beings be used to constitute a divide between people? Do they designate personal qualities? Why are socioculturally constructed characteristics correlated with biological sex? Is there really an essential connection between reproductive difference and gender roles?

3. While genital differences between embodied persons exist, sociocultural factors are more influential on incarnate subjectivity. Chromosomes are the basis for sex distinction, and thus we have male and female body kinds. But chromosomes are not responsible for all that we designate as "masculine" and "feminine." One major problem with complementarity anthropology, something underscored well by contemporary theologian Susan Ross, is that it does not allow sufficiently for historical and social constructions of gender.

4. Complementarity anthropology presumes difference first, beginning with what separates women and men. Separation and sexism have often functioned together with deleterious effects. Does an emphasis on woman as "receptive" and man as "active" contribute positively to the total development of women? This is unlikely, and it doesn't contribute to the holistic development of men either.

The square pegs of complementarity simply don't fit the round holes of existential life. Thus, complementarity breaks down in the face of a caricature of women as sweet and neat, compassionate and good at nursing and men as tough, outward-bound, and good at fighting. The fact is that there are lots of broad-shouldered, bearded men who are sweet and neat, and yes, good at nursing, and plenty of peachy complexioned soft-spoken women who are rough, tough, and very driven.

Some people claim that *complementarity* and *equality* are not mutually exclusive. While the terms themselves may not be so, the "effective history" of the notion of complementarity (to borrow a term from Hans-Georg Gadamer that refers not to "the idea" per se, but to the way the idea plays itself out historically) suggests otherwise. In historical practice, complementarity often has given rise to hierarchical ordering. Complementarity continues to be used today as the anthropological grounding for arguing against women's access to full leadership and sacerdotal ministry in the Catholic Church.

In short, a complementarity anthropology leaves me with too many troubling and unsatisfactory questions: Can we really give the chromosomal difference of sex so much ontological meaning? Whose designations of the differences between women and men are these in the first place? What function do they serve? Who benefits and who suffers? I conclude with Rosemary Radford Ruether that the anthropology of complementarity is not value free, that it does little to promote relations of mutuality and less for equality.

Looking toward the "equality" side of this equation, I find myself wanting to nuance the existing option by adding an insertion—"equality with distinctness." I construe distinctness in plural terms, as something that applies not only to different chromosomes resulting in different sexes, but to multiple dissimilarities between women and men that have been socioculturally influenced. I appreciate the comments of Elaine Graham, who reminds us that women's distinctiveness has emerged "strategically rather than ontologically" from a desire to develop alternative ways of knowing and to be in solidarity with others in order to survive and to thrive. In other words, it is probable that large numbers of women do have greater awareness of physical contingency than men; this is because of woman's particular social conditioning, the roles she has been cast in, and her making her way in these roles. It is likely that many women are better listeners than men; after years of being associated with the ear and the heart, with men being linked with voice, this is unsurprising. The heavy influences of social conditioning cannot be dismissed.

Considering the options offered in this symposium's subtitle, I stand on the side of the question that favors equality rather than complementarity. But I have concerns about this standpoint as well precisely because of how the notion of *"equality"* has functioned. I wish to offer two caveats.

In the choice for equality, it is essential that differences, in *plural* rather than singular form, not be liquidated. Diversity should never be collapsed for the sake of unity. And "equality" between women and men cannot be based on some diminishment of the importance of the body, as has sometimes happened when bodiliness has been reduced to a mere social construct. There is a natural givenness to human bodiliness, even while that givenness is socio-culturally interpreted and expressed. It is best that we begin with that givenness, the sameness we share as embodied persons, before moving to name differences and to construct complementarity. Historically we have begun with differences as defining. This has been to the detriment of women and the seeming advantage of men, though ultimately it is to the detriment of all.

I do question whether an equality anthropology highlights human *interdependence* enough. By forcing a choice between equality and complementarity, we have set unfortunate limits on the larger issue of *embodiment*. Should our primary purpose in looking to the body be the establishment of differences between women and men or the ruling out of such differences? We do not want to miss the insights that closer investigation of our common human bodiliness yields.

An analogy here may be helpful. For hundreds of years, Christian theologians interested in the relationship between the human and the rest of the created order began from the standpoint of difference, looking for what it was that distinguished the human from the rest of creation. Recently, theologians such as Kathryn Tanner, Dennis Edwards, and Sallie McFague have begun urging something else. They suggest that we begin with sameness, with our common creaturehood as trees, deer, grasses, humans, fish, birds, plants. A vastly new theology of creation is coming into view as a result.

I propose that we too choose an alternative strategy regarding our question at hand. Instead of probing the body for what it suggests about the differences between women and men, let us begin with the multiple strands of wisdom that might lie within our common human bodiliness. This requires consideration of bodiliness as a standpoint of *common ground.*

This choice is not an attempt to collapse the distinctiveness of persons, but rather an opportunity to place distinctness in the larger context of a supple unity, one that allows distinctiveness to appear as *a common feature of shared bodiliness.* Starting with the body as *common ground*, we together turn toward the rawest, most relational, vulnerable, and finite part of ourselves, ironically the place where God has opted to pitch God's tent. What *do* we hold in common as embodied persons?

To begin with, human bodily lives are subject to a shared set of biological stages; we are born, grow, persist for a while, and die. These are common physical realities that every body struggles to understand, to be reflective about, and to engage meaningfully. In addition, we can speak about ways in which society and culture inscribe our human bodies, molding persons' experiences for good and for ill. All of us prefer to be aware of this conditioning rather than naive about it. What is being inscribed on our ways of being bodily by consumerism, sexism, racism, classism, and ageism? What do we want to be "written" on these bodies and what do we wish to resist?

Another common feature of being bodily is the possibility of bringing consciousness to it. The interpretations we have of our bodies and the decisions we make regarding our level of engagement of the body shape our experience of it. Meaningful interpretation of ailing bodies, aging bodies, infertile bodies, impotent bodies, menstruating or menopausal bodies, for example, affects our presence in the world. And the kinds of choices made regarding specific ways of engaging the body in the world contribute to a sense of human identity.

We can speak most meaningfully of the common ground body in the context of a lived faith. Here it becomes possible to recognize the body as the location where relational life with God is lived and felt, where desire for God is ever manifest, and where finitude and incompleteness point us all toward otherness. Human bodiliness is our placedness within the large womb of God, and it simultaneously is what enables us to hold the mystery of divine life "within."

Bodiliness is where we humans claim to "hear" God, "see" God, "grasp," "sense," and "feel" something of God. It is the sacred space that makes it possible for us to speak in common about "stirrings within," "inner proddings," "recognitions of what compassion requires." This is not something male or female, but *human*, so very human *and bodily*.

Starting with *the body as common ground*, distinctiveness emerges, but it emerges second. It is a distinctiveness that doesn't separate persons, because we have recognized first our radical sameness and interconnection. The body as common ground invites a lifting up of every human body, not one body for this, and another for that—a lifting up of a common corporeality, acknowledging it as the place in which relational exchange with God, others, and creation can be known in "marrow bone" (Yeats).

We can expect to encounter God's spirit in these human bodies, as black and brown, white and red, young and old, womanly, manly. Insofar as this becomes an increasingly conscious reality, we, in all our plural distinctness, align our voices with all those on earth, proclaiming with the poet T. S. Eliot that truly "the hint half-guessed, the gift half-understood is incarnation."

## References

Butler, Judith. *Bodies That Matter: On the Discursive Limits of Sex.* New York: Routledge, 1993.

Cahill, Lisa Sowle. *Sex, Gender and Christian Ethics.* Cambridge: Cambridge University Press, 1996.

Cooey, Paula M. *Religious Imagination and the Body: A Feminist Analysis.* London: Oxford University Press, 1994.

Diprose, Rosalyn. *The Bodies of Women: Ethics, Embodiment and Sexual Difference.* New York: Routledge, 1994.

Edwards, Denis. *Jesus and the Wisdom of God: An Ecological Theology.* Maryknoll, N.Y.: Orbis Books, 1995.

Eliot, T. S. *Four Quartets.* New York: Harcourt Brace Jovanovich, 1943.

Gadamer, Hans-Georg. *Truth and Method.* New York: Seabury Press, 1975.

Graham, Elaine. *Making the Difference: Gender, Personhood, and Theology.* Minneapolis: Fortress, 1996.

Jones, Serene. *Feminist Theory and Christian Theology.* Minneapolis: Fortress, 2000.

McFague, Sallie. *The Body of God.* Minneapolis: Fortress, 1993.

Ross, Susan A. *Extravagant Affections: A Feminist Sacramental Theology.* New York: Continuum, 1998.

Ruether, Rosemary Radford. *Sexism and God-Talk: Toward a Feminist Theology.* Boston: Beacon Press, 1983.

Tanner, Kathryn. *God and Creation in Christian Theology: Tyranny or Empowerment.* New York: Blackwell, 1988.

# Part 3

## Different Races and Cultures:

### Uniting or Dividing
### Women in the Church?

W OMEN DO NOT FORM a monolithic block in the church in the United States. As in society as a whole, they form groups divided by race and class with the lion's share of prestige and power going to those who are "white," that is, of European descent. When white women speak of "women's experience" without listening to the experience of poor women or women of color, they commit the same pernicious error that they criticize men of having practiced: taking one's own life and making it normative. As one author ruefully observed, "all the women are white . . . all the blacks are men . . . but some of us are brave" (Cherrie Moraga). We are brave and present all the while, though triply invisible and silenced through the confluence of sex, race, and class.

Difference among women has become a powerful theme in feminist theory. For the classical mind-set, difference betokens something "other" that has to be assessed as better or worse. It also usually signals disruption, division, lack of unity. But women theorists argue that ignoring the difference of race and class between women presents the most serious threat to the mobilization of women's joint power. For women of color, owning difference allows for a liberating uniqueness of identity that is not just a repetition of dominant norms. For women who are dominant, however unself-consciously, within a cultural system of white supremacy, meeting and respecting difference among women who are their equals, neither inferior nor superior, allow for new patterns of relating that can affect the very future of our earth. In the words of the poet Audre Lorde, "difference is a raw and powerful connection."

In dialoguing about what kind of church women hope for in the twenty-first century, it is imperative to hear the voices of diverse women. Women of color and poor women, suffering and struggling against multiple oppressions, dream of a church whose transformed dimensions escape the notice of the white majority. At the same time, the latter need to be converted from the social sins of racism and ethnic prejudice in order for the church to be more truly and graciously the bearer of the good news of Jesus Christ. The insights of womanist, that is, African American female theologians, along with *mujerista*, that is, Latina thinkers, challenge and enrich the vision and fidelity of the whole church.

White Catholic ethicist Barbara Hilkert Andolsen analyzes the social injustice of white supremacy, rooted in racial or ethnic bigotry, as a sin that cries to heaven. Despite feeling humiliated and defensive when our own prejudice is uncovered, white, non-Hispanic women need to see such unmasking as the work of God's grace and to begin to take more responsibility for speaking out in all forums against the evil that so demeans whole groups of people. Black Catholic theologian Diana Hayes bores in on the horrors of slavery and its damaging, long-lasting aftermath. By supporting not only slavery but also misogynism, the church historically failed to live up to the gospel mandate that affirms the shared humanity of all as God's good creation. Now the provocative discourse of black women, doubly stripped of dignity by ecclesial racism and sexism, shatters the complacency of the deaf white church with a word calling for a house of God with "plenty good room" for all to sit down. Hispanic sociologist Ana María Díaz-Stevens brings the consciousness of community-based rather than individual-based life to her paper. Relegated to second-class status in parishes and church organizations, the Hispanic community suffers ongoing marginalization. All Catholic women are denied reception of *all* the sacraments, but Latina women, because they are marginalized, receive a double dose of ostracism. Her paper rings with the call to overcome fear of one another in favor of sharing our gifts and our needs.

During the discussion it was noted that it was a sign of hope that the *oppressors* were talking about this issue. A number affirmed the recommendation that white women should companion African and Latina women by raising the issue of racial injustice even though it was not their own direct experience. Disagreement arose over the idea that the oppressed need not be held to the same tone of civility in their discourse as those who have the advantage: Is honest expression of anger legitimate, or is reasonable argument more persuasive? While they appreciated the depth of pain experienced by women of color, some considered that too much emphasis was being placed on what divides women rather than on what unites them. Frustration, sadness, discouragement, and guilt over continued racism in society and church took the wind out of the sails of some participants. For others, such as a young adult who worked with poor, sick individuals and families of color, the exchange reinforced her commitment to this ministry. The speakers presented a united front— Who would be in favor of racism? The challenge, therefore, was to the hearts of individuals present and to the mental and sociological practices of racism that continue to poison the church.

—E. J.

# 6

## The Grace and Fortitude
## Not to Turn Our Backs

### BARBARA HILKERT ANDOLSEN

*You fear your children will grow up to join the patriarchy and tes-*
*tify against you, we fear our children will be dragged from a car*
*and shot down in the street, and you will turn your backs upon*
*the reasons they are dying.*

—Audre Lorde[1]

WHEN I BEGAN THIS ESSAY, these remarks from Audre Lorde sprang immediately to my mind. Lorde was a black feminist poet and theorist. This quotation has remained in my memory for more than twenty years because it taps into two important things we had in common. But, at the same time, the words profoundly challenge me with respect to the racism that divides us. Audre Lorde and I shared a commitment to feminism and we shared the experience of mothering a son. So when I read her statement, it took root deep in my conscience.

Too often, after a brief flurry of media coverage, we white women in the American Catholic church turn our backs on the

reasons why African American youth are brutalized and killed by
the police. We turn our backs on the reasons why African American babies are more than twice as likely as white babies to die in
infancy.[2] We turn our backs on the large numbers of young black
men and women dying of AIDS or locked up in our prisons. We
also turn our backs on the reasons why Hispanic young people are
much less likely to graduate from high school. We turn our backs
on the reasons why "so many [Puerto Ricans] are among the poorest of [New York City's] poor."[3] We turn our backs on the reasons
why Mexican day laborers are assaulted and almost killed in Farmingville, Long Island.[4]

The prominent African American ethicist Father Bryan Massingale has charged—with good reason—that American Catholic ethi-
cists have failed to address race relations as a major moral issue.
While the church has been a little better on Hispanic concerns, his
accusations should also give us pause in thinking about Latino
issues. Massingale indicates that even when the church makes a
statement on black issues, the church's concern is "often only passing, *ad hoc,* sporadic, incidental . . . and therefore totally inadequate given the key role of the ideology of white supremacy in
shaping American public life."[5]

Social injustices rooted in racial or ethnic bigotry and hatred
need to be a high priority on the social agenda of Roman Catholic
church women and their church in the twenty-first century. In this
respect, I was very disappointed when I checked the web-page of
the U.S. Conference of Catholic Bishops. I was aware of the bishops' excellent statement on racial justice, "Brothers and Sisters to
Us," but that is more than twenty years old.[6] The Bishops' Committee on Black Catholics issued a statement on the tenth anniversary of "Brothers and Sisters to Us," but I have not been able to
locate any major church pronouncements on the topic of racism in
more than a decade.[7] I checked the web-page for the Conference's
Department of Social Development and World Peace. There was a
list of key domestic issues—important topics worthy of our serious attention—such as children's health, welfare policy, and
hunger. In the fall of 2000, there was no listing for African Ameri-

can, black, race, race relations, or racism. There was a listing for immigration and refugees, but no listing for Hispanic or Latino issues, no listing immediately indicating Puerto Rican or Mexican-American concerns.[8] After all, Puerto Ricans are not immigrants; they are U.S. citizens. Some Mexican-Americans are descended from families that were living in the Southwest and California even before those areas were annexed to the United States. So Puerto Ricans and many Mexican-Americans are not immigrants.

It is sometimes said that the teachings of the Catholic Church on social justice are a well-kept "secret." The American Catholic bishops' admirable statements on racism from the 1960s and 1970s are an even better kept secret. Massingale's phrase "passing, *ad hoc,* sporadic, incidental . . . and therefore totally inadequate" echoes in my mind.

In this short piece, I want to lift up social sin as a particularly useful concept found in the social teachings of the Catholic Church. In 1971, Catholic bishops from around the world met at a synod where the topic was "Justice in the World." The official summary of the meeting indicates that the bishops "stressed again and again that the faithful, particularly the more wealthy and comfortable among them, simply do not see *structural social injustice as a sin,* simply feel no personal responsibility for it and simply feel no obligation to do anything about it."[9]

Racism and ethnic prejudice are two major forms of social sin. These are forms of social sin that many white, native-born Catholics "simply feel no personal responsibility for . . . and simply feel no obligation to do anything about." Many white Catholics can say truthfully that they have searched their consciences, and they find in their hearts no individual ill-will toward others merely because of race or ethnic origin. Aware of no personal animosity toward African Americans or Latinos, they conclude they have no personal responsibility for racism and, therefore, no obligation to work actively to end racism and ethnic bigotry.

Contemporary Catholic social teachings have something important to say at this point. Sin is not exclusively the result of actions over which specific individuals have control. Sin is also manifest in evil choices made by groups of people in society—choices to enhance the comfort and power of their own group at the unfair expense of others. Groups sin when they use religious, cultural, social, political, or economic power to maintain their social dominance. Personal evil and collective evil often become solidified in lasting patterns of social injustice. Then sin has an enduring presence in human communities. Social sins become entrenched in social structures that confront persons from socially disadvantaged groups with unwarranted obstacles to personal development and social participation.

Pope John Paul II has found the concept of social sin helpful when discussing racial and ethnic discrimination. In his 1999 Apostolic Exhortation *Ecclesia in America,* John Paul II—writing in conjunction with the bishops of North and South America—said racial discrimination is among the "social sins which cry to heaven." The pope continued: "The memory of the dark chapter of America's history, involving the practice of slavery and other situations of social discrimination, must awaken a sincere desire for conversion leading to reconciliation and communion" (§58).[10]

In the interests of recognizing diverse theological viewpoints within the church, I acknowledge that Pope John Paul II has articulated a view of social sin that is somewhat different in emphasis from the approach that I have just briefly outlined.[11] His view is discussed especially in the Apostolic Exhortation *Reconciliatio et paenitentia* (Reconciliation and Penance). His approach to social sin has a somewhat more ambivalent tone than the one I am presenting briefly here. John Paul fears that undue emphasis on social sin might undermine the crucial need for individuals to confront their direct, personal responsibility for sin. Thus, he insists: "Sin, in the proper sense, is always a personal act, since it is an act of freedom on the part of an individual person and not properly of a group or community" (*Reconciliatio et paenitentia* 16).[12]

Still, the pope is quick to point out that distorted social and cultural influences may "incite" a person to sin and that personal sins wound the sinner's relationship with her or his community. John Paul discusses relationships among large social groups that offend against "the plan of God, who intends that there be justice in the world and freedom and peace between individuals" (*Reconciliatio et paenitentia* 16). As I have already mentioned, the pope views patterns of racial and ethnic discrimination as important examples of the profound social wounds that sin inflicts on groups, communities, and nations. He acknowledges that the causes of such massive social evils are hard to identify. In such situations, responsibility seems "almost to become anonymous" (ibid.).

However, the pope asserts that if one speaks about such destructive social phenomena as "social sins," then the speaker should be understood to be making an analogy. John Paul returns immediately to his basic contention that the analogical use of the term "social sin" should "not cause us to underestimate the responsibility of the individuals involved. It is meant to be an appeal to the consciences of all, so that each may shoulder his or her responsibility seriously and courageously in order to change those disastrous conditions and intolerable situations" (*Reconciliatio et paenitentia* 16). Thus, to apply John Paul's thought to the question at hand, American Catholic women must not interpret the labeling of racism and ethnic bigotry as social sins to mean that Catholic women can evade personal responsibility for the struggle against racism and ethnic prejudice.

Throughout its entire history, white society in the United States has constructed social barriers that have unfairly limited the life possibilities of African-American citizens. In specific historical ways, U.S. society has erected hurdles that diminished the life chances of Mexican-Americans, Puerto Ricans, and those who came here from other countries in this hemisphere. The concept of social sin challenges us—white, non-Hispanic Americans—to acknowledge these barriers and to accept our moral obligation to work together to demolish the unjust social obstacles that impede full African American and Hispanic participation in our society—and our church.

The concept of social sin also indicates dramatically that the more privileged persons living in an unjust situation are also profoundly diminished by their participation in structures of social

sin. As theologian Donal Dorr says: "People can be oppressed by
structures of the mind—by distorted value-systems and patterns
of action . . . by inherited prejudices and insensitivities. Indeed this
kind of imposition is especially serious because it makes a person
less human in ways that he or she may be quite unaware of. So
there is a need for liberation from this oppression of the human
spirit."[13] White, non-Hispanic Americans need to be liberated
from the social sins of racism and ethnic bigotry. These sins are
particularly insidious because they make us "less human in ways
that [we] may be quite unaware of."

The good news of the Catholic faith is that liberation is at hand.
God loves us although we are sinners. God loves us although we
are participants in structures of racism and ethnic prejudice. God's
grace frees us to become new persons liberated from our sinful
prejudices.

Painful confrontations about racism and ethnic prejudice are
an element in God's saving work in America today. God's call to
conversion can be heard in the "angry" cries of the oppressed.
"Called to Be Catholic," the founding document of the Catholic
Common Ground Initiative, says "all of us will be refined in the
fires of genuine engagement." Nowhere are the "fires of genuine
engagement" hotter or more difficult to endure than in the areas of
race and ethnicity.[14]

The humiliation and the defensiveness that many of us experience when our unconscious racism or ethnic prejudice is uncovered are a necessary, although very painful, part of God's gift of
healing from our sins. Many of those difficult moments when
racism and ethnic prejudice are unmasked are signs of the Spirit's
redemptive work in the church and the world. On a more practical level, the burden of doing the Spirit's work of unmasking the
sins of racism and ethnic bigotry should not always fall on African
American women and Latinas. It takes a very heavy personal, professional, and social toll, when—as one of the few black women or
Latinas in a group—you are forced to be the one who is "always
dragging race or ethnicity into everything." To be designated per-
petually as the expert on racism and ethnic stereotyping is yet

another unjust burden imposed upon African American women and Latinas in a society deeply tainted by prejudice.

We white, non-Hispanic women have to take more responsibility in this regard. Racism and ethnic prejudice are our problems, and we must be the ones who take ongoing responsibility for addressing these evils. I am not suggesting that we ought to condemn other white women with a moral smugness that suggests that we (the critics) have surmounted racism and ethnic prejudice. Rather, we need humbly to address these sins in a way that admits our own sinfulness and our own need for God's forgiveness and grace.

Speaking out more often about racism and ethnic prejudice is one example of the works that follow from a true conversion from our sins. In other words, conversion requires an active reorientation of our lives. Specifically, it is morally irresponsible to remain paralyzed by the guilt feelings that accompany our recognition of our racism and ethnic bigotry. Indeed, a prolonged guilty paralysis is another way to ignore racism. A guilty stance of resignation—there is nothing I can do to end racism—is a temptation to which our religious education leaves Catholics unnecessarily vulnerable.

In our religious education, we need to hear stories of Catholic women and men who struggled valiantly against racism. I was tantalized by a brief comment in an issue of the Catholic Common Ground Initiative's newsletter, *Initiative Report,* that contained a description of a program at St. Vincent's Parish (Philadelphia) to confront racism. The article mentions an episode in 1912 when black Catholic children in the parish were required to take places in the end of the line when they approached the communion rail during their First Holy Communion ceremony. The story continues: "disheartened Black members, with the help of Mother Katherine Drexel, petitioned for and founded their own church, St. Catherine of Siena." Mother Katherine Drexel was an upper-class, white woman. How did she come to be an ally of these black Catholic parents? What can we learn from her more than fifty years of work on behalf of Native Americans and African Americans? We need to take hope from hearing the stories of Catholic forebears—like the soon to be canonized Katherine Drexel—who preceded us in the battle against social sin.

With God's grace, we have made progress in the struggle against racism and ethnic intolerance. In the lifetime of today's speakers, Jim Crow segregation has been ended. Partly as a result of affirmative action, many more blacks and Hispanics have moved into middle-class, professional positions. During the fall of 2000—a time of economic prosperity in the United States—unemployment was at a historic low for blacks and Hispanics. (However, the relatively low black unemployment rate is still more than twice the rate for whites. Hispanic rates are also significantly higher than the overall white rate, but significantly less than black rates.) We need to acknowledge the social progress that we have made. For one thing, this progress gives us evidence that, through dedicated struggle, change is possible.

We have made progress in diminishing the social sin of racism and its terrible consequences, but there is still much more to be done before ours will be a society that genuinely provides "liberty and justice for all." There is still much to be done before our church will be a clear sign to the world that every person is made in the image of God.

The genuine dialogue that the Catholic Common Ground Initiative seeks to promote requires trust. It is my experience that trust among white and black Catholics, among non-Hispanic and Hispanic Catholics is possible only when the more privileged participants show a constancy of purpose in struggling against racism and bigotry.

I close by urging, in the twenty-first century, that Roman Catholic women pay renewed attention to the virtue of fortitude as a key moral trait equipping us to battle the social sins of racism and ethnic bigotry. I have turned my attention to fortitude because it is that cardinal virtue that permits us to remain steadfast in the face of difficult moral challenges. I have in mind particularly that aspect of fortitude known as perseverance. Among my most cherished hopes for the twenty-first century is that the Roman Catholic Church will consistently face up to the evils of racism and ethnic prejudice. To use an African American phrase, we who are the church need to "keep on keeping on" in the struggle against racial discrimination and ethnic prejudice. Fortitude is manifest in a continual readiness to struggle against racism and ethnic prejudice in all their everyday permutations. When Father Massingale criticized the church's "passing, *ad hoc,* sporadic, incidental . . . and therefore totally inadequate" response to HIV/AIDS in particular, and racism in general, he was rightly denouncing the church's lack of fortitude.

If we cooperate with God's grace offered to us today, we will have the fortitude to chip away at the barriers of racism and ethnic bigotry. What I hope for American Catholic women and our church in the twenty-first century is that we will no longer turn our backs on the reasons the children of African American and Hispanic women are suffering and dying.

## Notes

1. Audre Lorde, "Age, Race, Class and Sex: Women Redefining Difference," in *Sister Outsider: Essays and Speeches* (Trumansburg, N.Y.: Crossing Press, 1984), 119.

2. Chart: "Infant Mortality Rates by Race and Hispanic Origin of Mother," available at http://raceandhealth.hhs.gov/3rdpgBlue/Infant/k2.gif. Accessed August 23, 2001.

3. Mireya Navarro, "Puerto Rican Presence Wanes in New York," *New York Times,* February 28, 2000, p. B7.

4. For accounts of the assaults and the underlying ethnic tensions that they revealed, see Charlie LeDuff, "Immigrant Workers Tell of Being Lured and Beaten," *New York Times,* September 20, 2000, p. B1; and Christine Haughney, "Assault on Mexicans Shakes Long Island Town: Suspects Linked to White Supremacists," *Washington Post,* November 28, 2000, p. A3. See also "A Climate of Fear: Latino Laborers Say They Face Daily Abuse by Residents," *Newsday* (Nassau and Suffolk Edition), August 26, 2000, p. A5. Catholic Charities was part of a coalition that supported a hiring center that would have brought the Mexican day laborers off street corners and offered them a variety of legal, health, and educational services. Necessary county funding was voted down after a fierce political battle. See "Focus of the Debate: Farmingville Finds Itself in Center of National Struggle," *Newsday* (Nassau and Suffolk Edition), May 20, 2001, p. A3.

5. Bryan N. Massingale, "A Public Theology, Black and Catholic: HIV/AIDs IN U. S. Communities Of Color" (paper presented at the annual meeting of the Catholic Theological Society of America, June 2000). [Used with author's permission.]

6. National Conference of Catholic Bishops, "Brothers and Sisters to Us: U.S. Bishops' Pastoral Letter on Racism in Our Day" (Washington: United States Catholic Conference, 1979); also available at www. osjspm. org/cst/racism.htm.

7. Bishops' Committee on Black Catholics, "For the Love of One Another: A Special Message on the Occasion of the Tenth Anniversary of Brothers and Sisters to Us" (Washington: United States Catholic Conference, 1989). For an insightful discussion of the strengths and limitations of recent statements by individual bishops, see Bryan N. Massingale, "James Cone and Recent Catholic Episcopal Teaching on Racism," *Theological Studies* 61 (December 2000): 700–730.

8. There are separate web-pages for the United States Catholic Conference's Departments for African American Catholics and for Hispanic Affairs. However, these sections are concerned primarily with internal church issues. Racism and ethnic prejudice and discrimination are social evils that ought be considered major social concerns of the whole church, not special concerns of African American or Hispanic Catholics.

9. Quoted in Peter J. Henriot, S.J., "Social Sin and Conversion: A Theology of the Church's Social Involvement," *Chicago Studies* 11 (summer 1972): 118.

10. Note this irony: in decrying the sin of slavery, John Paul uses darkness, that is, blackness, as a metaphor for evil.

11. Although I cannot discuss it at length here, I should note that John Paul also warns against an excessive concentration on social sin that could further discourage reception of the sacrament of Reconciliation– which normally requires individual confession of personal sin to a confessor.

12. Available at www.vatican.va/holy_father/john_paul_ii/apost_ exhortations/ index.htm.

13. Donal Dorr, *Option for the Poor: A Hundred Years of Vatican Social Teaching* (Maryknoll, N.Y.: Orbis Books, 1983), 203.

14. For an excellent example of the challenges involved in, and the commitment required for, genuine dialogue about race, see Richard Taylor with the assistance of LaVonne France, "Racial Healing at the Parish Level," *Initiative Report: Catholic Common Ground Initiative* 4 (September 2000): 3–6.

# 7

## Speaking the Future into Life:

### The Challenge of Black Women in the Church

#### DIANA HAYES

THE HISTORY OF CLASSICAL CHRISTIAN THEOLOGY has been one in which European and Euro-American males have been transformed not into images of God but into gods themselves with consequent authority over their earthly kingdoms, which were created and blessed by God: church, nation-state, workplace, and family. In other words, a masculinized European and Euro-American worldview has made male domination in the form of a patriarchal, hierarchical system normative. Women, persons of color, and all others outside that norm have been relegated to subordinate roles of passivity, surrogacy, and, with respect to persons of color, non-humanity.

This history and its affirmation by Christian doctrine and tradition are increasingly well known, albeit not fully accepted by all. This hegemonic worldview persists despite efforts by those "others" to limit or overcome its influence. We thus find ourselves today, because of the significant political and economic gains made by these "others," in a situation of backlash, especially in the United States, where white males and those historically privileged see themselves and their positions as threatened. The result has been an all-out assault on programs, agencies, institutions, and ideologies believed to support the shift to a more egalitarian sharing of power among women, persons of color, and others marginalized and oppressed in U.S. society and globally. The Christian churches, especially the Roman Catholic Church, are deeply implicated not only in the perpetuation of a patriarchal worldview but also in the regressive efforts to roll back time and circumstances to a gloried past that, in actuality, never truly existed. This is because these churches have, historically, failed to live up to the gospel mandate, which affirms the shared humanity and kinship of all as God's creation.

## HISTORICAL OVERVIEW

The subordination of women to men in the church was, in part, based on dualistic Neoplatonic understandings of body and spirit as set forth by Augustine and other church teachers, which left women with no right to control their own bodies, minds, offspring, and even their very souls. However, these interpretations took an even more sinister turn when applied to black bodies and minds, whether male or female.

Proponents of the Christian religion in the United States developed a tainted theology, which, in order to support the enslavement of African and other peoples, distorted the teachings of Jesus and Sacred Scripture. "Their theology itself propagated white control and black subservience as the normative expression of the Christian gospel. . . . whites employed the authority of the Bible in a self-serving and racist interpretation."[1]

In response to economic demands for cheap labor and the need of Euro-Americans to distinguish between that labor and themselves, persons of African descent, whether male or female, were dehumanized, while persons of European descent, especially males, were elevated to little less than gods.

> Whites viewed slaves like other livestock. . . . God had created and intended for them to work for their white masters with a cheerful and loyal countenance.
>
> The white man believed he replaced the mediating and liberating role of Jesus Christ. As the anointed Jesus, the white man possessed

omnipotent and salvific capabilities. For black chattel to reach God, then, whites forced African Americans to accept the intermediary and divine status of the white race.[2]

In so stating, I am not attempting a hierarchalizing of oppressions or engaging in the fruitless debate regarding the relative significance and/or heinousness of sexism over against racism or classism. I am merely noting that under the patriarchal system of Western society, women were relegated to lesser positions of subordination, while women of color and their men were denied their actual humanity and relegated to the status of chattel property.

Both natural law and Sacred Scripture, especially the teachings of Paul, were and continue to be used to support sexism, racism, classism, and homophobia. Church leaders interpreted the Scriptures to support the invalidity of women's leadership roles in all societal realms and the mandated enslavement of African peoples. As a result of its global influence of almost two thousand years, and recognizing that some of these understandings were derived originally from pre-Christian sources, the fact remains that Christianity was critically instrumental in supporting and fostering the development of misogynistic, heterosexist, homophobic, and racist ideologies which taint the teaching and spread of Christianity to this day.[3]

In the colonies of the Americas, this worldview was expanded to support the growth and flourishing of the Atlantic slave trade. The same hierarchical pattern used to subordinate women and the poor in Europe was used to formulate a theory of race that placed certain Western Europeans at the pinnacle of humanity and Africans at its lowest rung. Where slavery had existed for centuries throughout the world without any particular reference to race or skin color, this soon changed, as a scriptural foundation was provided for the "peculiar institution" of slavery found only in the New World, which relegated a person to the status of chattel property because of skin color or lineage.

At the same time, the rights and freedom of white or European and Euro-American women were further restricted by the development of the myth of True Womanhood. In keeping with this stereotype, white women, placed on a pedestal of perfection, found that that same pedestal was also a prison designed to deprive them of the freedom to live their lives as they desired. Yet the white woman was still all that a black woman was not, which resulted in barriers between them that have not been overcome to the present day. White women were seen as repositories of virtue in need of constant male protection, while black women were denied any positive attributes and seen as either asexual mammies whose sole joy in life was taking care of their mistress's children or immoral Jezebels whose rampant sexuality was uncontrollable. Where the white family was cast in rosy colors with the stern but loving *paterfamilias* at its head, the black family was seen as nonexistent and inherently dysfunctional.

Black women during slavery were stripped of their children as soon as they were weaned and of their husbands, the fathers of those children, at the whim of the master or the mistress. The master was often the cause of physical and emotional abuse of the female slave, especially if she gave birth to a child who too closely resembled the master, overseer, or sons of the plantation. She was stripped of life, dignity, and selfhood, all that makes one human.

> . . . for every part of the black woman was used by him. To him she was a fragmented commodity whose feelings and choices were rarely considered: her head and her heart were separated from her back and her hands and divided from her womb and vagina.[4]

Today, black women's bodies are still considered the property of others, as are the bodies of Latinas and poor white women. They are often sterilized without their knowledge and required to use contraceptives in order to obtain social services or aid. They are often required to deny the existence of the men in their lives in order to retain those benefits and to find work, regardless of how menial or poorly paid, without any assistance for their children, who are subsequently left home alone and then taken by the state as "abandoned or abused." This cycle of dehumanization continues to this very day.[5]

As a result, the experience of oppression by African American and other women of color and that by Euro-American women, from the inception of slavery in the American colonies to the present day, has been vastly different. Ironically, the former have often had greater access to employment—albeit restricted in nature—to education, and to other opportunities because they are seen as less threatening than their men. Today, women of color are fighting several battles at once. They are fighting for the right that should have been theirs at birth not to be discriminated against because of their race, class, and gender. Theirs is not and has never been a struggle simply against sexism but one waged against the multiplicative oppressions of gender, race, and class united in one single body. These differences continue to serve as an obstacle to women seeking to unite over shared difficulties. The words of Joyce Ladner, written in the 1970s, still ring true:

> much of the current focus on being liberated from the constraints and protectiveness of the society which is proposed by Women's Liberation groups has never appealed to Black women, and in this sense, we have always been "free," and able to develop as individuals even under the most harsh circumstances. This freedom, as well as the tremendous hardships from which Black women suffered, allowed for the development of a female personality that is rarely described in scholarly journals for its obstinate faith and ability to survive. Neither is its peculiar, humanistic character and quiet courage viewed as the epitome of what the American model of femininity should be.[6]

The latter view is one not often lifted up in the black community. The religious body that has in many ways been both liberating and oppressing for black women is the black church, which, while proclaiming human freedom, at the same time continues to bind women in stereotypical roles adopted from dominant society, continuing rather than challenging their continued enslavement.

## THE BLACK CHURCH

A religion originally of the poor, women, slaves, and the marginalized, which promised a salvation both physical and spiritual, was paradoxically used both to dehumanize and to foster in those so treated an acceptance of their degraded state. The scriptural curses of Cain and Ham's son, Canaan, were invoked both to indoctrinate and to "pacify," creating better slaves. However, other scriptural passages, especially those in the book of Exodus and the Gospels, were read by the slaves as texts for liberation and hope for freedom, both physical and spiritual.[7]

The black church operated, in the South especially, as an "invisible institution," one which existed literally at the margins of plantation society, as blacks gathered clandestinely in forests, coves, and river hollows to proclaim their faith.[8] The very text used to perpetuate slavery, the Holy Bible, was used by the slaves themselves to contradict their masters' interpretation. While the former saw themselves as taking the place of Christ for their slaves,[9] handing down laws and judging their conduct, behavior, and right to live, the slaves discovered language in the Bible that enabled them to recognize and depict their masters as betrayers of God, especially the one they knew had come as a liberator, Jesus the Christ. For them, their faith was something to "lean on," something that would help them "get through" the horrors of slavery, not by submitting to their masters' every whim but by constantly rejecting his/her authority over their lives. Their songs, stories, prayers, and sermons highlighted God's creation of them as a people worthy of respect and their oppressors as false prophets and heretics.

These churches, whether in the North or the South, were places of refuge for blacks, who therein could acknowledge their humanity and God's affirmation of it and therefore of their human dignity as bestowed by God. The black church was born as a sign of contradiction in the United States, one that proclaimed a Christian message of radical liberation and redemption. At the same time, that same church could also serve as a hypocritical site of passivism, sexism, colorism, heterosexism, and homophobia. The same spirit of liberation that found a home in the black church was, at times, stifled and rejected in favor of a survivalist mode of living, which put greater emphasis on life after death than freedom in the present world.

Sojourner Truth, former slave, Abolitionist, and Suffragette, reflected upon this contradictory stance:

> I know that it is hard for men to give up entirely. . . . I was amused how men speak up for one another. They cannot bear that a woman should say anything about the man, but they will stand here and take up the time in man's cause. . . . Men has [sic] got their rights, and women has [sic] not got their rights. That is the trouble. When woman gets her rights man will be right.

Jacquelyn Grant and other womanist theologians have acknowledged the black church's contradictory stance as one in which the critical role of women, as the backbone of the church, was recognized. Grant also notes, however, that this usually meant that they were relegated physically to the back of the church, to the kitchens, the women's clubs, and the pews, any role and location other than that which would give them authority over men. In other words, like white women, black women were rendered invisible and silent in the black church. This was a position they vehemently rejected.

The black church of today has changed little from this stance. Black ministers are in the forefront of the Christian churches that denounce black gays and lesbians and women as a group in the ordained ministry. Although many of the Protestant churches now acknowledge and affirm black women's calling to preach, teach, and proclaim the gospel, once ordained, many women find themselves once again marginalized, given small, poor churches, placed only in administrative positions or as associate pastors under several men.

Kelly Brown Douglas, in critiquing the sexism and homophobia of the black church, asserts:

> White culture's sexual characterization and exploitation of Black people has had a far-reaching and deleterious impact on Black lives. This attack has provided a gateway for the contamination of all of Black sexuality, from Black peoples' relationships with themselves to their relationship with God. But perhaps the most insidious result of the White cultural attack upon Black sexuality is that it has rendered the Black community practically silent in terms of sexual discourse.[10]

A Womanist Discourse of Liberation

It is largely because of the failure of today's leading liberation theologies to include the voices and experiences of women of color
that a new call for recognition has emerged in the United States.
That voice is African American; that voice is womanist. Originally
grounded in Alice Walker's paradigm-shifting definition of the
term "womanist,"[11] the womanist movement, at least in its earliest
manifestation as a theology of liberation, has moved beyond
Walker to articulate the characteristics of a black woman's way of
being in the world, which challenges the restricted and privileged
understandings of liberation put forth by feminist and black theologies.

Womanist theology has emerged as both a critique of existing
theologies and a mediator for the emerging articulate, religiously
grounded voice of African American women in the dwindling
years of the twentieth century. In their efforts to discover, uncover,
and recover roles and images, histories and stories, visions and
dreams of their foremothers in the United States and Africa, they
challenge the common understanding of what it means to be black
(male) and female (white). In addition, womanists grapple with
issues of class, as too many black women, especially those who
head their families alone, exist below the poverty line in the United
States and are being targeted as the cause of societal problems of
which they are, in actuality, the victims.

At the same time, they shatter the complacent image of the
black church, revealing its inability to serve as a vehicle of liberation within the black community without undergoing significant
changes in its self-understanding and self-proclamation. Womanists, therefore, in their provocative discourse, challenge the uncrit-
ical sexism and heterosexism/homophobia that has made itself at
home within the bosom of the black church, calling it to account
for its claims of serving as a vehicle of freedom. As Jacqueline
Grant affirms: The failure "of the Black church and Black Theol-

ogy to proclaim explicitly the liberation of Black Women indicates that they cannot claim to be agencies of divine liberation."[12]

## Black, Catholic, and Womanist

As a womanist, I am concerned about and committed to the survival of an entire people, male and female, gay, lesbian, and straight, physically and/or mentally challenged, and of every race and ethnicity. I believe that my rights as an African American woman are guaranteed only when the rights of all are guaranteed; that my liberty is restricted when that of another is restricted; that my human dignity is denied when that of others is trampled into the dirt. I believe that no one can be free until all are free.

As a Roman Catholic womanist theologian, I seek to explore the intersection of race, class, gender, sexuality, and religion in an effort to reveal the role that the Christian religion, especially my own faith, has played in affirming, exploiting, perpetuating, and upholding understandings of these social constructs that have served to provide not only a language but a pervasive, hegemonic ethos of subordination and oppression of women and persons of color. Grounded in the Neoplatonic dualistic separation of the sacred and secular worlds, such an understanding has enabled the spread of a race-based hierarchical/patriarchal system that supported the enslavement not just of other human beings but of other Christians, the subordination of women and the dehumanization of persons of color, and a stance that today still supports rather than challenges the oppression and marginalization of so many.

The challenge is to look at these social constructs, including religion itself as it has come to be constituted in the United States, through eyes opened by the recognition of the "other-createdness" from which they emerged. Dualistic systems allow for the emergence of an "either/or" understanding of life, knowledge, morality, and society. It enables the differentiation of human beings into "us and them," into "human and nonhuman," into those we recognize as friend and "others" by whom we feel threatened. It speaks a coldly sterile language of negativity, dualism, separation, subordination, and alienation.

Patricia Hill Collins speaks of black women, especially those now in professional fields, as "outsiders-within."[13] Our positions as women with degrees at the master or doctoral level, especially in institutions of higher learning, provide us with an insider's position, able to participate to a certain degree in academic discourse and to have an impact on others in those institutions. Simultaneously, because we are black women or women of color, we are also "outsiders" whose views are not always welcome and whose input is often trivialized. We find ourselves straddling two worlds, that of academia or other professions, and that of the black community with its often very different perspective. In order to belong truly to one world, it is assumed that we must give up our existence in the other since they are not complementary. Too often these assumptions, however, are cynically grounded in issues of power, control, and manipulation. Ironically, our experience as women of color within the church is quite similar.

> The exclusion of Black women's ideas from mainstream academic discourse and the curious placement of African-American women intellectuals in both feminist and Black social and political thought has meant that Black women intellectuals have remained outsiders within all three communities. The assumptions on which full group membership are based . . . whiteness for feminist thought, maleness for Black social and political thought, and the combination for mainstream scholarship . . . all negate a Black female reality. Prevented from becoming full insiders in any of these areas of inquiry, Black women remain outsiders within, individuals whose marginality provides a distinctive angle of vision on the theories put forth by such intellectual communities.[14]

Black women, as the bearers of their community's culture, have, historically, been the forgers of new ways of being and speaking in the world. They recognize with Collins that "[p]rivatizing and hoarding ideas upholds inequality. Sharing ideas through translation and teaching supports democracy."[15] It is our task today to speak the future into life, a future inclusive of all. We do so by working to redefine what it means to be male and female in language that complements the actual experiences of those engaged in living out maleness and femaleness, in ways inclusive of both heterosexual and homosexual understandings. In our stories, songs, prayers, and God-talk (theologizing), black women speak life into being, not a stunted growth unable to flourish and condemned to premature death, but a life that is fruitful and representative of a diversity created not by human hands but by divine ones.

Black women have, historically, worked to make community, a desire deeply rooted in their African ancestry and made even more important by their experiences in the United States.

> "Making community" means the processes of creating religious, educational, health-care, philanthropic, political, and familial institutions and professional organizations that enabled our people to survive. In the early eighteenth and nineteenth centuries, black women . . . made community . . . through the building and shaping of slave culture. Later the process of "making community" was repeated in post-emancipation agricultural areas and then in urban industrial societies. . . . It was through "making community" that Black women were able to redefine themselves, project sexual respectability, reshape morality, and define a new aesthetic.
> . . . Black women came to subjecthood and acquired agency through the creation of community.[16]

Today we who name ourselves womanists continue in our efforts to "make community" wherever we find ourselves. In so doing, we are creating a new language of liberation that is open to any and all who are willing to speak plainly without assuming that their language will give them power and/or authority over another. As womanists, we see as our challenge the gathering of the myriad threads of the richly diverse black community and breathing into it renewed life, which can serve as a model of life for our world. That model is centered on the co-createdness of all, regardless of efforts to separate them by the arbitrary use of divisive language which restricts rather than encourages the fullness of life and its possibilities. All who are oppressed share in solidarity with each other, a solidarity that should not be laid aside for individual desires or "battles." The struggle is communal, not individual, and can be won only if experiences are shared, stories are told, songs are sung, histories are reclaimed and restored, and if a new language emerges that speaks words of peace and unity, unites, and recalls both the pain and the joy of our different heritages.

As Christian women who believe in our God-given right to become whoever and whatever we are capable of becoming, womanists challenge not only the black Christian churches but all of Christianity to live out the true, liberating message of Christ, for the truth will set us all free. To be a Christian is to be about the salvation of the world, not through forced conversions, not through the oppression of those who differ in skin color, gender, religion, economic status, or sexual orientation, but through somehow loving a new world into life, a world in which all people can live free. We must live the life we sing about, challenging ourselves to never be reconciled to any doctrine or ideology that renders us less than human, silent and invisible. We must dismantle the master's house, if necessary, using new tools forged from our own discovery and recovery of our long lost and stolen pasts as women of every race and nation and build a house of God that has "plenty good room" for all to sit down.

## NOTES

1. Dwight Hopkins, *Shoes That Fit Our Feet: Sources for a Constructive Black Theology* (Maryknoll, N.Y.: Orbis Books, 1997), 21.

2. Ibid., 22.

3. Diana L. Hayes, *Hagar's Daughters: Womanist Ways of Being in the World,* The 1995 Madeleva Lecture in Spirituality (Mahwah, N.J.: Paulist Press, 1995), 86–90.

4. Barbara Omolade, *The Rising Song of African American Women* (New York and London: Routledge, 1994), 21.

5. Kelly Brown Douglas, *Sexuality and the Black Church: A Womanist Perspective* (Maryknoll, N.Y.: Orbis Books, 1999); Dorothy Roberts, *Killing the Black Body: Race, Reproduction and the Meaning of Liberty* (New York: Vintage Press, 1997), 56-103; Linda Gordon, *Pitied But Not*

*Entitled: Single Mothers and the History of Welfare* (Cambridge, Mass.: Harvard University Press, 1994).

6. Joyce Ladner, *Tomorrow's Tomorrow: The Black Woman* (Lincoln, Neb.: University of Nebraska Press, 1971; repr. 1995), 280.

7. Hopkins, *Shoes That Fit*, 22–35; Hayes, *Hagar's Daughters*, 32–40; and Albert Raboteau, *Slave Religion: The "Invisible Institution" in the Antebellum South* (New York and London: Oxford University Press, 1978).

8. Raboteau, *Slave Religion*.

9. Hopkins, *Shoes That Fit*.

10. Douglas, *Sexuality and the Black Church*, 85.

11. Alice Walker, *In Search of Our Mother's Gardens: Womanist Prose* (New York: Harcourt Brace Jovanovich, 1983), xi.

12. Jacqueline Grant, *White Woman's Christ, Black Woman's Jesus: Feminist Christology and Womanist Response*, American Academy of Religion Academy Series 64 (Atlanta, Ga.: Scholars Press, 1989), 331.

13. Patricia Hill Collins, *Black Feminist Thought: Knowledge, Consciousness, and the Politics of Empowerment: Perspectives on Gender*, vol. 1 (New York and London: Routledge, 1990), 11–13.

14. Ibid., 12.

15. Ibid., xxiii.

16. Darlene Clark Hine, *Black Women and the Reconstruction of American History* (Bloomington and Indianapolis: Indiana University Press, 1994), xxii.

# 8

# The Divine Danger of Diversity:

## A Hispanic Catholic Perspective

### ANA MARÍA DÍAZ-STEVENS

N OT TOO LONG AGO a visiting priest walked down our center aisle after the reading of the Gospel with a simple message: "Don't judge a book by its cover." The cover is only outward appearance, and though not totally insignificant, it is in the last analysis incidental. Though it can give you a glimpse of what lies beneath, it is limited in its revelation. It takes all of a few seconds to take a glance at a cover; it takes much longer to read and understand the book's contents. I must confess that I find this an old, tired phrase. But if truth be told, our visiting priest was correct. Do we penetrate the cover to understand how the same things that bring us together—our common beliefs and social needs—can also keep us apart? Do we understand that the level to which we need and have attained these things may be different not only for individuals but for whole groups of people, and that this, in turn, may affect the level of acceptability of one group for another, and the relationship of the core society with distinct groups?

Our assignment today was to look at things that separate and unite us as women in the church. Coming from a tradition where the needs of the family and the community are privileged over personal needs, I have opted to look at the question from the perspective not merely of the individual but of the collectivity. I can stand here and give you a laundry list of the things that are the same for all of us: the need to be cared for and loved and to reciprocate in kind; the need for family and friends; the need for a means of livelihood; the need for a roof over our heads, clothes on our backs, and education for ourselves and our children; the need for a means of maintaining our health; the need for a healthy environment where we can live peaceful and meaningful lives, where we can recreate and share our gifts and present our needs, cares, and aspirations without fear of discrimination or refusal. We all need a place to meet each other with not just tolerance but acceptance.

But there are other variables that I know separate me from others in very concrete terms: my native language, my culture, my nationality or place of birth, my social class, my multiracial reality, my level of education, my profession, my immediate neighborhood, my city, my state, my region of the country, my religion, my family and its traditions, my ethnic background, my personal beliefs and values, my migration experience, my idiosyncrasies, my personal aspirations, and even my prejudices. And the list could go on, for we are very clever at recognizing and even inventing differences. But the truth of the matter is that the things that separate us in our society and even in our church are not always figments of our imagination or the "mere cover." Rather, they are the real story, made up of substantive, real things. And though, to an extent, all these differences and distinctions are socially constructed, cultural differences are real: different life experiences such as those wrought through migration, cultural and religious differences, age differences, differences emanating from disabilities and capabilities, gender differences, and racial differences are all too real.

So let me be clear: I am not here to excuse, negate, or belittle the reality of these things and their attendant consequences. There is no getting away from reality. Hurt feelings, the sense of ostracism or humiliation one suffers on account of one's standing within a group, an organization, a society, are as real to us as the air we breathe. That all these things are not tangible does not mean they are not there. I know this for a fact—a fact based on lived experiences and scars too stubborn to heal. I find it difficult to understand, for example, the second-class status to which parishes I have belonged to have relegated the Puerto Rican and Hispanic community. The same may be said in terms of my gender. If I am a full member of the church, why then, I ask, does the church deny me one of its sacraments based on the fact that I am a woman rather than a man?

But, in dealing with my hurt and the obstacles I encounter in life, I am often reminded of something my father, of blessed memory, would often say: "Beware! If you are not hurting at least a little, it is because you are dead": *Es un peligro estar vivo.* Acknowledging that "it is indeed dangerous to be alive," I focus today on our response to our human and social conditions from the perspective of our membership in the Catholic faith. I would like to talk about the joy and the pain, the life-giving gifts and the scars that one bears as a member of the Catholic Church and as a person living in this society. It is easy for me to go into my parish church and tell you what is wrong with it—meaning what I do not like, what hurts or does not suit me. It is relatively easy to look at my church, the Catholic Church, and simply proclaim: "When it comes to women or when it comes to Hispanics they just don't get it" perhaps because "we are judged by the cover."

But that Sunday in my parish church, Father's simple words made me reflect on my own responsibilities and not just on the shortcomings of others. I simply asked myself if I, too, had a propensity to find fault and easily judge other groups—the entire church, for that matter—without giving myself enough time to discover and rediscover certain things about those I was prejudging. I came away with this very simple but real conviction. I guess there is something good in recognizing shortcomings, ours and those of others. If we do not recognize what is wrong, we will not be able to correct mistakes or to know that there is room and even need for improvement. After all, we are all supposed to be seekers of perfection. But when naming what is wrong becomes my only preoccupation, when it becomes my obsession, when I criticize things as they are as if I, or my particular group, were outsiders exempted from participation in and therefore responsibility for what has taken place and is still taking place, then there is a problem.

It is not as easy to see ourselves for what we really are. It is difficult to acknowledge how our actions or complacency has affected others. We always find reasons to blame others rather than ourselves. In my husband's family, an often-used phrase meant to diffuse tension is "It's Gary's fault." Gary, being the youngest of three brothers, often took the blame because his brothers thought their parents would forgive him because of his inexperience. In my own family, Juan, my oldest brother, was the one who took the blame most often, for the opposite reason: He was older and more experienced, and, therefore, was supposed to watch over us and be our model. So today, when we do not want to talk about something that did not go as planned, we resort to the old phrases: "It's Gary's fault" or "Blame Juan." Of course, this has become a joke. We don't really mean it. Or do we? Are we still excusing ourselves by making light of the responsibility we should bear for our actions? Are we trying to say that we are incapable of what we consider "Gary-" or "Juan-like" blunders?

As a member of the Catholic Church, the "Gary" or "Juan" in my life may be a group of newly arrived members who seek equal standing with me and my group, a particular priest, a sister, a fellow parishioner, or simply the entire hierarchical structure of the church. And while I do not mean to excuse the institutional church and its hierarchy from its many excesses, I am simply stating that as a Hispanic and as a woman I must recognize that it takes more than a particular priest or sister, or even the entire Irish hierarchy in this country and the curia in Rome to put the church in the United States in the condition in which it finds itself today. I must face reality: It is always easier to blame somebody else, claiming either, on the one hand, their lack of experience or, on the other, that they should have known better. Ultimately, however, I cannot go through life blaming "Gary" or "Juan" for my own lack of love, understanding, and prudence.

As a general statement, I claimed earlier that what has kept us apart in the church are the very things that ought to unite us—our gifts and our needs. Consider among our many and wonderful gifts those of unique languages, cultural and religious traditions, music, and so on. You may say these are differences, and I would agree with you. But just because they appear as differences does not mean they are not gifts. These gifts that we have and that in some way are unique to each one of us also engender certain needs and responses from others.

Take language, for instance. Rather than belittle other people's language, would it not be better for us to encourage them to learn other languages while keeping their own? When you say, "Now you are in America you must learn English," are you forgetting that America encompasses more than the United States? Catholicism was first brought here by those who spoke Spanish: Does that mean that those who arrived later—those who spoke English—should be deprived of the right to speak their language? When people say that newcomers must learn English, is it because they want to share something with them, because they want the newcomers to have a better opportunity for education, employment, and so on or because the newcomer's language is seen as inferior and worthy of extermination? Just as we force a language upon others, are we willing to learn new languages ourselves, recognizing that our reality is in fact multiracial, multilingual, and multicultural? Do we understand that people share diverse identities —that we can share commonalities with a diversity of cultures, traditions, languages, and even races?

Often what is at stake is not so much what we want people to do as how and why we want people to act in certain ways. For example, we perhaps all agree that there is a need for people to celebrate their faith through religious traditions. But when we look at the way these traditions are observed concretely, such as La Festa di San Genaro or La Fiesta de San Juan, or Saint Patrick's Day celebrations, do we rejoice and join in the celebration or do we poke around for negative things to say: "They are too rowdy; this is just an excuse for getting drunk; look at the garbage they left behind"? Thus, another thing that keeps us apart is our lack of tolerance and appreciation for other people's gifts. We have not embraced diversity.

When I was finishing my doctoral course work at Fordham University, the late Father Joseph Fitzpatrick would bring a stack of books to his class on "American Assimilation." He would read a short passage from each one of them and then ask the members of the class to identify the group of people referred to in each passage. Invariably the students would say, "Negroes or Puerto Ricans," perhaps because the passages depicted the subjects in a very negative light. Who else could the authors be speaking about? To the students' amazement they were speaking about the Polish, the Germans, the Irish, the Italians! These passages were "the cover" in which these groups were wrapped. There I realized that oftentimes "the cover" we see around other people is nothing but an old image of ourselves that we want desperately to cast off. Mistakenly, we think we can free ourselves of our negative image by making others assume or wear it.

It never ceases to amaze me that people who have suffered much are, oftentimes and at the least provocation, the ones most likely to inflict suffering on others. In the face of others' suffering haven't you heard it said: "When we came to this country we had to learn the language, work in cold factories, live in dilapidated buildings. Who do they think they are? They must pay their dues just like we did"? In other words, "How dare they aspire to a better life?" Or "What do they expect from us—to help them to better education, better housing, better working conditions than the ones we had?" In terms of religion this may translate into, "So they want to use the upper church and to compete with us for the church resources. They should know their place—and until they prove themselves that place is in the basement." I have also heard from others: "Just because they have been here longer, they think they have the answer to every question. They are just jealous because we have not given up our culture the way they have." Thus, our own pain is often manifested in a false sense of pride and self-righteousness, which in turn engenders lack of compassion and understanding.

I come to the last and perhaps most important reason why we keep ourselves apart—FEAR! Fear of others, fear of the circumstances, fear of the future, fear of the unknown, and fear of becoming informed lest it elicit a serious response or some sort of commitment from us; in short, fear of the consequences. Judging by our actions we must be very insecure people. Otherwise, why would we think that letting others assert their identity would take away from or undermine ours? We ask ourselves, What will others think of us if we let all these newcomers with all their strange customs and ways of life into our parish? If we embrace them, what is the cost we must pay? If we share our resources with them, how much will be left for us? Will we lose control, our good image, our sense of dignity, our direction? If there is something history has taught us, it is that this line of reasoning has been present not only at the personal or parish level.

The institutional church in the United States historically has made some very damaging decisions on the basis of political expediency. After all, the church is not only a religious institution but a social institution as well. As a social institution the church has sought to maintain its clout in society sometimes to the detriment of its Christian call to perfection. For the longest time the institution of the Catholic Church in the United States had to struggle against such things as nativism and the prejudice of a society based on an Anglo-Saxon Protestant matrix. As parishes were burned, Catholics were excluded from public office and housing; health and sanitation services were curtailed for the Catholic population. Catholics saw themselves forced to claim and prove their loyalty to this country by emphasizing the need for "Americanization." There was fear of being treated differently because this meant not only discrimination but often open persecution. The idea was to make sure that the message went out and was heard loud and clear that Irish, German, French, Polish, and Italian Catholics in the United States were first and foremost American citizens. This reasoning and acting prompted some authors to ask what may be deemed by some to be a very impertinent question, but one that, nonetheless, has some bearing on the subject we are discussing here today: Has the church been more American than Catholic?

When Protestant England invaded Catholic Ireland, the Catholic Church stood by the Irish. When Russia and Prussia invaded Poland, the church stood by the Polish Catholics for their national rights. But when the United States invaded Mexico and Puerto Rico, the Catholic Church told us to stop being Latinos. Has the church indulged in pious colonialism? Will the Euro-American members of the church continue to impose their pattern of assimilation upon these groups, reasoning that what was good for them is good for Native Americans, Asian Americans, African Americans, and Hispanics? Will this desire to "keep business as usual" and to use one size to fit all continue to determine the policies of the church even when these groups outnumber all others? And will the misnamed new groups perpetuate in part this pattern? Will Mexican Americans, for example, exact adherence to a Mexican American way as the norm for all other Hispanics? Will they become the Irish of the Hispanic church? Will Puerto Ricans see the Dominicans and Central Americans as "basement-church" parishioners? Will Hispanics fight for the scant available resources with African Americans and Asian Americans, claiming that Hispanics were here first?

In other words, will complacency, stubbornness, pride, lack of compassion and understanding, and fear continue to rule our judgment? Will we continue to judge each other by the cover, by mere appearances, without getting to the heart of the matter—that we are all children of God, members of one faith, entitled to justice and dignity, to love and acceptance with all our uniqueness, our distinctiveness, our needs and our gifts? On the other hand, if, through God's grace and our own effort, we learn from past experiences, good and bad, if we open our hearts to each other in a spirit of love and sacrifice, the outcome of our action and our labor will be freedom from the sins of fear and ignorance that have enslaved us and kept us apart. Only then will we make of our church what it claims to be—a rich experience of universality where everyone, no matter his or her origin or life condition, is indeed welcome among us, as a member of the body of Christ, equally graced and redeemed by Christ's blood, and thus most certainly worthy of our interest, our love and our acceptance.

ADDENDUM

As regards what divides us as women in the church, I understand that others may choose to underscore the issue of gender or differing theological positions or nuances. Although gender is always an issue, I have found that in dealing with people of different socioeconomic groups and ethnic and/or racial backgrounds, at the practical everyday level, oftentimes the divide is greater in terms of these variables of class, race, and ethnicity than in terms of theological positions or gender issues. However, in trying to understand the responses of particular groups, one must take into consideration that these variables are not isolated from one another. A person or a group does not live a compartmentalized existence. It is possible, and is often the case with some non-Euro-American groups, that the behavior exhibited is not the one expected by their social and economic counterparts in the Euro-American community. You may find Puerto Ricans and other Hispanics who may be very liberal, and even radical, when it comes to political and social action and to the social teachings of the church but at the same time are rather conservative regarding questions of the church's magisterium and doctrinal and moral issues. It is often the radical attachment to one that makes it possible to be radically attached to the other. For example, the fact that I as a Puerto Rican Catholic feel radically in favor of an option for the poor, labor unions, the right of women to equal pay for equal work, sovereignty for all peoples, and freedom from interference and undue influence from stronger nations, and so on, may also lead me to question abortion rights and even the use of contraceptives, particularly when I know how the United States used Puerto Rican women to test contraceptives that were not deemed safe for U.S. consumption and when approximately 40 percent of all Puerto Rican women of childbearing age have been sterilized, sometimes without their proper consent or knowledge of the consequences. There is a question here of free choice for women to control their bodies. But this choice has to do with their right to be fully informed so that the government cannot curtail their right to have offspring, rather than the choice of treating the fetus as an appendage that can be disposed of. Such an issue transcends the personal sphere since at stake may be the entire future of a people. Furthermore, it touches upon other issues, such as personal morality, ethics in government, ethics in the health professions, and such sociopolitical issues as economics and a people's right to self-determination. One may also ask, Where was the U.S. Catholic Church when Puerto Rican women were being sterilized en masse? We know that the two North American bishops to Puerto Rico during that era were recalled to the United States because of a heated religious and political debate over this issue. This was at a time when the Kennedy family was coming into power, and it seems as if some within the U.S. Catholic hierarchy did not want to call too much attention to issues that could be so controversial that they could endanger a Catholic candidate's position for the highest office in the land.

# Part 4

## *Women as Leaven in Church and Society*

O NE OF THE STRIKING SIGNS of these times is the emergence of women into positions of leadership in church and society. Both of these public areas reflect a long history of being shaped by men's needs and ways of acting. Business, politics, law, higher education, sports, entertainment, and all other zones of social endeavor now must accommodate women, who also have primary family responsibilities and needs that are specifically female. Do women yield to the necessity simply to conform to these structures the way they are? Or do they mount pressure to transform them, leading to a more humane culture? The metaphor of leaven, taken from the Gospel along with such images as salt and light ("You are the salt of the earth . . ." [Matt. 5:13]), raises this issue. The importance of taking a transforming stance grows even greater when the secular orientation of public culture is kept clearly in view.

Many participants found the metaphor of leaven objectionable insofar as it seems to imply that women are something added to church and society rather than being part of the substance itself. The question of the far-reaching effect of women's engagement in public life remains, however. The experience is creating a whole new set of "facts on the ground" that women and men are grappling with and that church life and teaching must take into account.

As leader of the Vatican delegation to the United Nations conference on women in Beijing in 1995, Mary Ann Glendon developed keen appreciation for the church's teaching on women's human dignity in areas of social justice. Her paper presents the argument that no other world institution speaks so eloquently on behalf of poor, abused, and marginalized people as does the Catholic Church. The fact that the faces of the poor are predominantly those of women makes the church a genuine ally of women's well-being and its teaching a challenge to a society that veers off toward individualistic satisfaction. Women need to examine whether they are changing or yielding to a culture that disrespects the life-forming, family roles of wife and mother.

As a member of Congress, Representative Marcy Kaptur is immersed in democratic practices of governance. Pointing to the gap between this experience and the way business is conducted in the church, her paper urges U.S. Catholic women to use American society's culture of freedom to move the global church toward democratic structures open to women. By contrast, keeping the voices of women mute in the church renders the church politically immature and thus less able to live out its world-transforming vocation. Her own words were buttressed by interviews she conducted with over one hundred Catholic women, a majority of whom expressed frustration with the current situation of women's secondary role in the church.

Discussion brought forth clear diversity. Some few believed strongly in the traditional roles of men and women in the church, with women's main contribution to the transformation of the world being made through their role as mother. A number were glad to hear the defense of church teaching about the dispossessed and the importance of family values. Even among these, however, the contrast between American civic and Catholic social experience surfaced. Why does the secular structure of autocracy seem more appropriate to the church than the secular structure of democracy? Is the former somehow more sacred? The church as a political entity and the church as a moral entity are intrinsically related. Mired in nondemocratic structures, how can the church speak to the world about the dignity of women? Many commented on the gap women experience between their subordinate place in church organization and the call to be influential in transforming society. The fact that women are increasingly educated also came to the fore. Their informed way of seeing the world leads them inevitably to discount a mentality that insists on obedience to authority without questioning.

Margaret O'Brien Steinfels, editor of the journal *Commonweal* and moderator of all the dialogue sessions, raised the question of how the credibility of the church is affected when its teaching about the marginalized in society is not reflected in its treatment of its own members. "How long can an institution preach one thing and yet internally not be able to observe the standards it is preaching? The church has to come to grips with this," she said. As some noted, the example of Jesus and his positive dealings with women without fear should encourage the church itself to become more conformed to the gospel. Otherwise, its moral positions regarding virtue and the social realm are compromised.

— E.J.

# 9

## The Challenge of "Being Leaven" in a Secular Culture

### MARY ANN GLENDON

IN THIS FOURTH MEETING on the general topic, "What Kind of Church Are American Catholic Women Looking Toward in the Twenty-First Century," Congresswoman Kaptur and I have been asked to offer reflections on "Women as Leaven in the Church and Society" in the light of the general theme—and to do so in the space of twenty minutes! That assignment brings to mind the Charlie Brown cartoon where Charlie and his friends are taking a history exam and the teacher says: "Discuss the origins of World War II. Feel free to use both sides of the paper." Fortunately, the role of the speakers at these gatherings is not to exhaust the subject, but just to get the ball rolling for discussion. To that end, we've been asked to state a position, and then to propose two issues within the topic for discussion. So let me begin with this proposition: *Catholic Christians don't have a choice about being "leaven."*

That was settled when Our Lord told us two thousand years ago that we must try to be like leaven in the loaf and lights upon a hill (Matt. 13:33). As that injunction has been understood in our tradition, it means we are supposed to make a difference in the earthly kingdom even though it's not our final home. It means that Catholic Christians simply do not have the option of just minding our own business and turning our backs on sinful society. Since Vatican II, the reminders of our evangelizing vocation have become so loud and clear that one would have to be deaf not to hear them.

The early Christians must have had doubts about whether they were up to such a daunting job, because we find St. Paul using the image of leaven to encourage them. "Don't you know," Paul tells the Corinthians, "that even a little yeast has its effect all through the dough?" (1 Cor. 5:6). But, as you recall, the Corinthians were a sinful and quarrelsome lot—just like us. So Paul has to remind them that bad yeast spreads all through the dough too (5:7). That is another way in which we have no choice about being leaven: The only question is whether we will be good leaven or bad leaven—whether we are helping to raise the social loaf, or whether we are inflicting a yeast infection on the body politic.

That proposition brings me to the first issue I would suggest for discussion. This issue is related to, but not quite the same as, a question that has arisen now and then in previous Common Ground meetings: Are we more American than Catholic? I would put the question this way: *To what extent are we being transformed by the culture, rather than transforming it?*

It seems to me that the chair of the Catholic Common Ground Committee, Archbishop Lipscomb, was right on the mark when he suggested in a recent speech that the relationship of American Catholics to the dominant secularized culture needs careful scrutiny. That problem is, of course, as old as Christianity. In Matthew's Gospel we find Jesus saying to his disciples, "Beware the leaven of the Pharisees" (Matt. 13:35). And when Paul wrote to the prosperous, self-satisfied Corinthians, he advised them: "Do not conform yourselves to the spirit of the age."

I think those warnings bring us to the heart of the problem of being "leaven" in contemporary American society. We have the good fortune to live in a prosperous nation with a great deal of individual freedom. But it is a nation whose culture is saturated with habits and attitudes that are antithetical to core Christian beliefs. It is a society steeped in materialism, consumerism, secularism, and moral relativism. It is a society where self-reliance slides easily into self-absorption, and liberty into license. It is a society where it is risky to allow oneself to be dependent, a society that is increasingly dangerous for those at the fragile beginnings and endings of life.

Fortunately, what Archbishop Lipscomb calls the dominant secular culture is not the only American culture. But it is the culture that reigns among the women and men who wield the most influence in governments, political parties, corporations, mass media, foundations, and universities. These movers and shakers, according to opinion studies, are less apt to have strong ties to religion and family life than most of their fellow citizens. That is hardly surprising, because the more one believes in self-sacrificing love, the more impediments one faces in trying to have a say about the conditions under which we live, work, and raise our children.

That brings me to the second point I would propose for discussion: *What can we do to increase respect in our society for women who want to give priority to the vocation of parenthood?* (I will speak here of women, but I want to note that the problem increasingly affects men as well.)

For centuries and still today, one of the main ways that women have tried to be a transformative presence in the world is through the nurture and education of children. For centuries and still today, those tasks have received too little respect. But who can doubt that they are among the most influential determinants of the supply and quality of leaven in any society?

Think for a moment about all the public meetings you have attended in recent years and ask yourself what proportion of those present were mothers of children under ten. I think you will agree that they are underrepresented—even at meetings on issues that affect them deeply. And being out of sight, they and their concerns are all too often out of mind. That is worrisome, for although we live in a time of unprecedented advances for women in economic and political life, women are facing new kinds of difficulties in the vocation that, for most of us, still offers our principal opportunity to make a difference, for better or worse, on our journey through life. In fact, the same period that saw women gain new opportunities to be influential in public life also saw a dramatic rise in the proportion of women in the poverty population, a shift that has come to be known as the feminization of poverty.

I call the difficulties to which I referred a moment ago "the four deadly Ds": Disrespect for work performed in the home; Disadvantages in the workplace for those who give priority to family life; the increased risk of Divorce, which makes it risky to give priority to family life; and the Destitution that afflicts so many female-headed households.

When a recent national poll asked women, "What is the main problem you deal with in your personal life?" the number one response was "worry about not having enough time and energy to get through their daily lives." Needless to say, when one feels that way, one is not going to attend many meetings. One is not going to find it easy to make one's voice heard on social and political issues. I cannot even count the numbers of young men and women I have known over the years who have declined offers of important jobs because they felt the toll on family life would be too great. I have always sympathized with their decisions, but at the same time I have regretted society's loss of their talents—and the underrepresentation of their points of view in public life.

Now I am supposed to try to relate the two problems I have mentioned to our general theme, "What Kind of Church Are American Catholic Women Looking Toward in the Twenty-First Century?" It seems right to begin by giving thanks for a church that has become the single most influential institutional voice for the voiceless in the world—speaking out on behalf of the poor, the vulnerable, and the marginalized. Hers is also one of the very few voices reminding us that social justice is not a policy or a program, but a virtue grounded in good moral character.

It is of course true that just as individual Christians can be caught up in the culture, so can congregations of individuals. That is why, although the church is always holy, she is always in need of purification. Living in a materialistic society makes it very difficult for some of her children to take to heart the church's teachings on social justice, especially the preferential option for the poor. Living in a self-indulgent society makes it very hard for some to accept the church's refusal to dilute her demanding moral teachings. Our love of liberty makes many of us bridle at the slightest assertion of authority. In short, we all like the parts of Catholicism that are easiest for us personally to put into practice. John Paul II warns against such a pick-and-choose approach. He writes that "Catholics should eagerly involve themselves as advocates for the weak and marginalized," but notes that a failure to defend unborn life "renders suspect any claims to the 'rightness' of positions in other matters affecting the poorest and least powerful of the human community" (*Evangelium vitae* 23).

I believe the church's history teaches that we do not serve any useful goal by being less than we are. If nothing else, the fact that the faces of the poor in America are now predominantly those of women should prompt us to think carefully about the *links* among exaggerated individualism, extreme liberty, moral relativism, the breakdown of the family, and the feminization of poverty. We can't get around the cross. It's a stumbling block to some and a scandal to others, but there it is.

That's why I believe that a saint for the twenty-first century will be Dorothy Day. She came to accept Catholic teaching in its fullness the hard way. In the 1920s, she pioneered, so to speak, in a lifestyle that would bring disappointment, degradation, and disease to countless young women when that lifestyle became common in later years. She became pregnant, was treated miserably by the father of the child, and at his insistence had an abortion. Then she cohabited with another man and had a child out of wedlock. When she finally turned her life over to God, her conversion was radical and complete; her gift of self was total; her love of the church was profound; and her influence continues to touch thousands of lives.

Another great sign of hope for the church in the twenty-first century, I believe, is the growth of her large, vibrant lay organizations. These groups with their different charisms really took off in the late twentieth century. Their rise, providentially, came at the same time that geographic mobility was taking a severe toll on traditional parish and neighborhood life. Just as the church has turned more and more to laywomen and men for roles that once were performed by priests and sisters, the great lay organizations have appeared, as if on cue, to fill the new needs of changing times. They are publishing magazines and newspapers; they are founding schools and universities; they are producing radio and television programs; they are ministering to the needy at home and abroad; they are serving as a kind of extended family to many young parents; and they are intensifying the Christian presence in politics, business, and professional life in many countries.

It is thanks to these groups, to no small degree, that the laity is no longer a "sleeping giant." The sleeping giant is awakening, and her many feminine attributes cannot be denied. Focolare, Communio e Liberazione, the Neo-Catechumens, Regnum Christi, and many more are pouring youth, strength, and vitality into the life of the church.

In conclusion, I would like to come back to the parable about leaven in Matthew's Gospel. Like the parables about the sower and the mustard seed that precede it, this one seems to emphasize that "being leaven" is God's mysterious work, not ours. The point of these parables seems to be that the kingdom of God grows in ways that are mysterious to us. That prompts one final reflection on our topic—that perhaps we should be cautious about identifying ourselves as "leaven," lest we forget who is really in charge.

# 10 ──────────────────

## *Politics, Religion, and Women*

### HON. MARCY KAPTUR

I N ANSWERING THE DIFFICULT QUESTION What kind of church do
American women want in the twenty-first century, let me reply:
I seek a church that more fully represents at its policy-making levels, and at every other level, those doing the work and those professing the beliefs. American women Catholics, blessed to live in a
democratic republic, have a particular responsibility to pull the
church forward internationally as a moral and political force to
dignify both women and men. Women's worth is a political value;
it is also a moral value. I do not expect miracles from the institutional church in broadening women's roles within the church,
though what a joy that would be. But I do expect steady progress
in our church, propelled by the "priesthood of believers" to move
the institutional "church" forward. Each of us bears responsibility
for this transformational calling. Compare my answer to another
woman, who, when I asked her this question, angrily blurted out,
"You mean you want women to be more than silent martyrs?"

In preparation for these remarks, over the last two years I have
interviewed over one hundred U.S. Catholic women from all walks
of life, asking them to reply to this question. I want to represent
their views more fully—women religious; practicing lay Catholic
women who are married, widowed, divorced, single; marginalized

Catholic women. Further, I encouraged any of them who were interested to write "Epistles" on this question. Their answers are excerpted in the "Consultation" that follows. As women of freedom, each of us holds a spiritual obligation to be vigilant in gaining women voice and representation in this new millennium.

To begin with, women are more than leaven, which suggests some additive to a body of milled grain that causes it to lighten or change its form through fermentation. Women are more than an "additive." Without them there would be no church, domestically or internationally. In fact, women make up the majority of the world's 1,018,257,000 lay Catholics. According to 1998 Vatican statistics, Catholics in the United States, who number 59,860,000, constitute 6 percent of that global total. Importantly, after Germany, the United States is the largest financier of Roman Catholic activity globally. Women's increased activism and engagement with church finances, at every level, are another important wall that must be scaled. Internationally, in terms of the church's "civil service," there are 814,779 nuns or women religious; there are 400,460 priests. Again, women outnumber the men two to one. In the United States, there are 83,624 nuns and 49,458 priests, approximately 12 percent of the world's total. Again, the *presence of women in service to the church is double their male counterparts' representation*. In the United States, 82 percent of parish lay ministers are women, according to a study conducted by the Bishop's Subcommittee on Lay Ministry by the National Pastoral Life Center in New York. In fact, *religious women*—as the sponsors and administrators of hospitals and health care facilities, educational institutions, and social service organizations—*are the largest employers of labor in the Catholic Church in the United States*. Religious women hire more workers than all of the bishops in the United States put together.

## Church History: Rooted In Empire

An old adage cautions that the two topics you absolutely must never bring up at a dinner party are politics and religion. So,

American women of the twenty-first century, let's break old molds! We're going to talk about politics, religion, AND women. Politics concerns more than elections. It concerns power. It concerns values. Politics results in the ordering of basic human relationships and whether those yield war or peace, equality or inequality, freedom or repression, justice or injustice. I want to touch on the confluence of politics and religion and how the former influences the latter, and how they jointly impact the dignity of women. I believe that as more societies in the world advance human dignity for all people, the Roman Church, if it wishes to survive, will necessarily be influenced by that progress. I only wish that the Roman Church would use its dignity-affirming creed to advance the cause of women more forcefully, internally and externally. But I recognize the political constraints on the church among the majority of the world's people who are not free. Those of us in free societies must do our part in helping pull the church forward, and all the world's people forward, to elevate the dignity of women and men, and their equal worth as God's creatures, part of the same Being.

A learned man once counseled me: "If you want to understand the way an institution functions, look to the year it was founded." Setting moral tenets aside, organized religion and politics—including the Roman Catholic denomination—always have been inextricably linked. Vatican City indeed has been an independent nation-state since the signing of the Lateran Treaty in 1929. It holds representation at the United Nations. It is a political creature, with a long history. Most recently, that connection between politics and religion was documented well by Carl Bernstein in his book *His Holiness: John Paul II and the History of his Time* (Penguin, 1997). Pope John Paul II's papacy and his life's work centered on developing an alternative to Nazi and Communist political ideologies, which tormented his native Poland and adjoining nations. History will record the collapse of those horrific political systems, which required fifty years of unwavering Cold War commitment by the people of the United States with our NATO allies, together with the unflagging commitment of the Vatican and this particular pope.

Finally, and no less significant, the ultimate collapse of the Berlin Wall came about because the majority of people in those Communist nations no longer believed the ideology. The political record of the official church, however, is mixed. For example, it is perceived as less admirable in its tepid defense of the Jewish people during the Holocaust in World War II, as recent news accounts have elaborated. In any case, we are discussing here a two-thousand-year-old institution that is a political force, which can and does employ political leverage for good or evil.

The Roman Catholic Church rests its institutional origins in antiquity, in the old world of the Roman Empire. Though its moral tenets are timeless, its administrative structures were given birth in autocratic societies, where women were regarded as chattel at best, and often as slaves and prostitutes. Indeed, concepts such as king, empire, lord, and kingdom were the working ideas of the time. These words easily weave their way in and out of the prayers that trace their origins to those times and which we still utter today. References to women were minimal. The church became a highly politicized institution, allying itself with emperors and kings, where civil rulers often would convert entire populations in nations where the subjects had no voice in self-governance, nor any free choice of religion. Mexico is our closest geographic example of this. The Spanish conquest of the native Indian populations in the sixteenth century, with the unsavory alliance of the church with the wealthy and powerful, remains why the Mexican Constitution born of revolution early in the twentieth century still outlaws so much clerical activity there and land ownership by any official church. This month, in fact, I am scheduled to visit a city in Mexico named Matamoros, which means "Kill the Moors," a clear sign of what happened in Spain centuries ago.

It is two millennia since the founding of the Roman Church. How do I, as an American woman born in the freedom of the twentieth century—subsequent to women achieving legal standing as "whole persons" with the right to vote, the privilege of obtaining higher education, and an identity not imposed by any outside controlling force—accommodate to the restricted administrative architecture of the Roman Church? After all, our rights as women are less than a century old, but the church has existed for over two thousand years. You and I know what life is like in free societies, more than the global church hierarchy does. We can learn from one another. Freedom's people have had to negotiate freedom. We have developed an instinctive reaction against closed thinking, inflexible administrative apparatus, and unrepresentative structures. We seek an authenticity that arises from the inherent merit and worth of the "being" or "enterprise." Living in a free, pluralistic society requires the development of behaviors that expand tolerance, share power, negotiate differences, resist autocratic strictures, and encourage self-discipline and actuation. It is not easy. But any day I would rather negotiate freedom than autocracy.

Day by day, as a servant of the people, I am engaged in proposing and passing laws that affect millions of people. However, my voice is muted relative to issues of concern in our church, except in forums such as this one. So I wish to deeply thank Cardinal Bernardin posthumously for this opportunity. My own life has developed in a way that I can now become what is called a "cardinal" [or chair] in the Congress of the United States, as the highest-ranking member of my party on the committee on which I serve. Yet religious and laywomen in the church cannot achieve any such rank within the hierarchy. It can be perplexing and dispiriting.

The road for women has been a long and tortuous journey. For most of recorded history, women have been regarded as "property." If women were even seen in public, they certainly were not heard, and they remain so in vast portions of the world. Even when our own nation was founded, women were not considered persons under our Constitution. That would not come for a century and a half with the adoption of the Nineteenth Amendment in 1920, granting us full suffrage rights. Women's words, their deepest thoughts, largely have been lost to history forever. Does it not trouble you that we have the Gospels of Matthew, Mark, Luke, and John, but not of Mary, Elizabeth, Martha, and Mary Magdalene? In the first millennium, the very "concept of woman" as an "autonomous being" had not been born. That would not occur until five hundred years later, and it found expression through the church. For example, Roman Catholic sisters of the St. Joseph order in sixteenth-century France were released from their convents by priests and allowed to minister to the poor of Paris, but *only* dressed in black veils and widows' garb. Why? Because the only women permitted on the streets unaccompanied in that age were widows, so as not to disturb the social constraints of the time. Thus, even the origins of sisters' habits are heavily tied to costuming strictures rooted in woman's bondage to a male presence, even a deceased male. Similarly, in 1600 in England, William Shaftoe gave his daughter Marjorie in marriage, along with a dowry of fifty sheep, to a suitor she had not chosen. This was the world of women's bondage half a millennium ago, just a blink of the eye as historians view the passage of time. These examples help us decipher the interlinkage of politics, culture, religion, and women's freedom and dignity.

Women of the church, at great sacrifice, have moved forward the dignity of all women. Jo Ann Kay McNamara in her book *Sister in Arms: Catholic Nuns through Two Millennia* writes:

> [Let us] call attention to our foremothers who, for two millennia, have broken new paths for women in a hostile and forbidden world. They served their god and their church. In doing so, they fulfilled themselves and laid a foundation for all women. Without the caring and sacrifice of these women, it is impossible to imagine the feminist movements of modern times finding any purchase in the public world. They created the image and reality of the autonomous woman—they formed the profession through which that autonomy was activated. They still devote their lives to the care and development of human beings everywhere.

Let us now turn to one of the most central documents of our faith to illustrate a similar point—the Nicene Creed—written in the fourth century at the Council of Nicaea (located in modern-day Turkey). That council was called *not* by a pope but by an *emperor*—Constantine, to be exact! Obviously, he was not a woman! Conveniently, he became the first emperor of Rome who was a Christian convert; he, in contrast to his pagan predecessors, allowed the church to exist. Again, the fusing of politics and religion is undebatable. As we repeat the words of this creed at every Mass, we hear the echoes of an emperor. Let us consider some of these words. They are unusual for an American to utter—King, Lord, Almighty. . . . In fact, in that prayer, there are at least twenty-four references to the "masculine," yet only one "feminine," where the Virgin Mary is mentioned. Words are important. They reveal thought. I have often asked myself, Why is the reference to "the Almighty," as opposed to the "All Loving?" Where is mention of "servant" and "service"? Why is mention made of "eternally begotten of the Father" with no mention of "Mother"? A subsequent council was called about four decades later by another emperor—Theodosius. More edits were added to the Creed we still say each time Mass is offered. And four hundred years after that, Empress Irene, Emperor Leo's widow, and her sons as the "real" heirs to the throne, had to call additional councils to address some of the church-related disagreements of the time, including whether veneration of images was allowed. The church and political leadership remained fused through very autocratic systems of governance.

Yet from Mary, the mother of Jesus, who remains his most perfect disciple who huddled in the room with the apostles after his crucifixion, we have no written record. Imagine a historical omission of this proportion! Women's words were not recorded because of their lack of standing. Women's worth is a political value; they were afforded none. Mary Magdalene, who first discovered that Christ had risen and to whom he announced his ascension, has no significant recorded words. In fact, her entire reputation down through history has been smudged in a way that bears no resemblance to reality according to the words of the New Testament. To be missing the words of these women, but simultaneously to have emperors call church councils producing words whose influence resounds to this day, is a profound conundrum to me. Frankly, for an American, even the hierarchy's garb—the vestments, the hats, often the regal colors—bears too close a resemblance to many of the trappings of empire. Symbols matter. I have been very pleased to note Pope John Paul II's use of the white shepherd's cloak in the majority of his public appearances.

Retracing this history has everything to do with women's standing in the new millennium. The Roman Church became rooted in a time of empire, with women as chattel, the property of their fathers, masters, or husbands, not considered important enough to be educated or recorded. The institutional state of the Roman Church today—and its political statements and deeds toward women throughout most of history—still reflect the "autocratic," as opposed to "democratic," and the vestiges of "empire" as opposed to "republic." The political lesson is obvious. The church's role in sanctifying monogamous marriage, so as to dignify women, and its declaration of women saints has moved history forward. Now this progress needs to be fully operationalized in the contemporary church context.

Another ancient story illustrates how the church of 1000 C.E. through its actions made political statements as well. Then it had none of the papal power structures we recognize today—"The Vatican," its several departments, the College of Cardinals, and so on. Christopher Bellitto writes in the December 1999 issue of *America:*

> Popes were stuck in quicksand: Rome's wealthy families jockeyed to put their favorite sons into office. It was one of the worst periods of instability in the papacy's history: 21 popes sat between 946 and 1048. At 18, John XII (955–64) was the youngest pope ever and died of a stroke, according to legend, while in bed with a married woman. One scholar calculates that one out of every three popes who served between 872 and 1012 died violent or suspicious deaths, some by mutilation, beating or suffocation. From 872 to 1054, only one pope left Italian soil.
>
> Popes did not even stick together. Stephen VI (896–97) infamously conducted the "cadaver synod," in which he tried the rotting corpse of his predecessor, Formusus, for perjury. The prosecutors found the dead pope guilty, stripped him of his regalia, cut off his blessing hand and dumped the body in the Tiber. In turn, the Romans deposed Stephen, who was strangled in jail. But these dramatic circumstances went largely unnoticed. Few people knew the pope's name.

Again, the church historically has been a very political human institution, forging alliances, sometimes for good, and sometimes for evil. As a circumspect woman reminded me, "Well, God must truly love the church to let it survive in spite of so many mistakes."

## THE FUTURE: THE CHURCH MUST MATURE POLITICALLY

For American Catholics, there remains this duopoly: *though the moral teachings of the church rest on one plane, its governing structures remain on another.* The pope is only infallible in terms of faith and morals, not political or administrative judgments. The role of women in society is a political judgment. For Americans, with our beliefs in "checks and balances" and shared authority structures, the church's internal governing structures create a tension between our democratic values and the church's stilted architecture.

To bring this point home, let me tell this contemporary story. One of my friends, who is a religious woman, was elected the representative of *all* women religious in the United States to the U.S. Bishop's Conference. I called to congratulate her and ask her what had happened at the first meeting. She told me it was a "lot like Congress. There are parliamentary rules to prevent people from speaking. So you have to ask permission to speak." I asked her when she asked permission, what it was she said before the bishops. She told me that I really didn't understand because, as an elected representative of all the women's orders in the United States, she is only allowed to attend as an "observer." She is not allowed to speak. I was absolutely stunned! What she told me is illustrative of the oversight of women that tragically occurs in our church too frequently. These are educated, faith-filled women who operate universities, hospitals, orphanages, schools, nursing homes, housing developments, charities, hospices, and so on. Many are pastoral administrators. The fact that she cannot speak harks back to the habits of empire, where "subjects" cannot speak, a behavior destructive to the human spirit and unjust.

Especially for Americans, because of our own revolution, we enshrine the concepts of liberty and equality that have liberated the people of our nation and indeed major segments of the world. We in the West kept alive the very concept of liberty for humanity during its twilight struggle with the forces of tyranny in the twentieth century. The citizens of the free world replaced kings, lords, Führers, and commissars with elected presidents and prime ministers. Masses of people gained dignity and became empowered through electoral reforms. Importantly, education became democratized. Only in the last century have woman begun their fresh, new page in history's political journal, as we too have become free, educated persons. In many cases, this has been achieved through the selfless service of Catholic women, religious and lay. In my mind, they are among the holiest, most sacrificial people I have ever met. Our church must recognize the worth of women—religious and lay—and properly include them within all church structures.

Indeed, the church must mature politically. It may never become democratic; even the United States is a republic, not a pure democracy. But surely the church's governing and administrative structures must become more inclusive and representative. It must better reflect human progress in the way it organizes appropriate governing structures, obviously with continent-to-continent sensitivity. Through its moral teachings, the church has endured historically. Now it must struggle with the products of some of its own handiwork—more open, civil societies that govern by a rule of law in which men and women share responsibility and dignity. The church must give voice to women in new ways. For example, it was a serious historical omission of the church not to allow women to study theology at the doctoral level until the last quarter of the twentieth century. The church must negotiate its ark not just in societies where the citizenry is subjugated politically, but in places where human possibility has never been as great due to political advances.

Someone asked me if this meant I believe in the ordination of women as priests. This is a hot-button question for many, and I personally hold no opposition to it. However, I am much more interested in who handles the finances of the Vatican, dioceses, and our churches. As a member of the Appropriations Committee of the Congress, I can attest to the relationship between money and control. If women had been in charge, could the financial scandals that plagued the Vatican have been avoided? John Paul II deserves a great deal of credit for moving to world accounting standards for the Vatican's finances. I can also tell you, it was a sister from Detroit who put those books in order. But, as you might imagine, she is only listed as a footnote in books detailing the endeavor.

Women in the church—lay and religious—should be able to achieve policy-making roles at all levels of the church's hierarchy, in its worldwide charities, in its institutions of higher learning, in the formation of Catholic thought, in its media and public relations, in the administration of the church structures on various continents, frankly even in the election of the pope. Women make up the majority of those doing the work and professing the beliefs. Why shouldn't they be included? The ceiling in the masculine-dominated Sistine Chapel was painted even before commissioned artists—all male—actually learned to paint the female body. That is why all the arms on the few women figures look masculine. It is now 2001. Isn't it time for history to move forward?

St. Paul in Galatians 3:28 reminds us "there is no longer male and female, for all are one in Christ Jesus." Cardinal Lopez Trujillo envisions a modern womanhood that can "integrate the essential aspects of the feminine condition, which include virginity and maternity, as the realization of the vocation to love and give of oneself." The challenge to the church hierarchy and the vast membership of the church for the new millennium is to embrace the feminine. As free women, it is our duty to help move the church toward oneness in being.

So let us pray that the priesthood of believers will be:

> More imbued with the Holy Spirit, more wholly holy;
> More loving, more wise, more just;
> More representative, less autocratic;
> More inclusive, less ecclesiological;
> More servantly, less Kingly and Queenly;

More unifying, less divisive;
More hopeful, less fearful;
More forgiving, less judgmental;
More respectful, less defensive;
More honest historically;
More shepherding, less royal;

Let us pray for a church that loves the poor, including the half of humanity it has marginalized for two millennia;

Let us pray for a church that is infused at all levels with its masculine and feminine substance.

AMEN!

# Consultation:

## Toledo Women Speak

T O PREPARE THEIR PAPERS for this Catholic Common Ground Initiative project, those presenters who are scholars consulted their books. Congresswoman Marcy Kaptur did what politicians do and consulted her constituents. The following excerpts are taken from letters written by women in her district who responded to her invitation to reflect on their hopes for the church.–E.J.

What kind of church am I looking toward in the twenty-first century? Or better, what kind of church do I look forward to for my three granddaughters? One where the walls have disappeared—where women and men can equally be called to the priesthood or to be the spouse of a priest, all being strong role models for my granddaughters. One where the walls between denominations continue to break down and good will and dialogue be built up. One that searches for ways to rethink women's sexual and reproductive issues. In face of disease, poverty, illiteracy, child abuse in the U.S. and more massively in the Third World, I hope the Catholic hierarchy will acknowledge that if we want to eliminate such horrors as partial-birth abortion, then we need to provide women with the information and means to avoid unwanted pregnancies.

I look forward to a church that will continue to move forward toward inclusiveness, not divisiveness. I am proud of how far we have come in my lifetime and hope we continue on the pathways opened up by Vatican II.

*Mary Schiltz*

I am a white female Roman Catholic, married for forty years (to the same man), with five grown children. I am critical of the title of this project, "American Catholic women." This term removes our thoughts from the head of the church, the pope, and the church's Magisterium. To me Rome where Peter, the rock, lived, is the headquarters of our church. Our church is guided by the Holy Spirit, the third person of the Holy Trinity. Therefore God is guiding our church through the successor to Peter, the pope, in union with the bishops. Because of this guidance in faith and morals, the church is different from a democracy.

There are many issues that face us in the twenty-first century. To me the gravest is the failure of many Catholics to believe in the true presence of Jesus Christ in the Holy Eucharist. Other issues are married priests, female priests, contraception, and abortion. A true Catholic knows what the Catholic church teaches about these issues. However, if in this twenty-first century the church changes any of these teachings, we as true Catholics must believe that this is God's will since the church is guided by God the Holy Spirit.

*Carol Elizabeth Duffy*

The Catholic church needs to do what it won't do—recognize women as full and equal partners with men and anything else is not worth discussing.

*Mary Lee Gladieux*

We have been taught even as children that we have free will and should think for ourselves. Consciences are both exercised and strengthened as we confront moral choices and act independently and responsibly. We not only have the right to make personal, domestic, professional, and civic decisions but also we have the responsibility to do so. . . . One of my concerns is that the "traditions" of the church do not encourage this growth.

No longer is the church, at least in developed countries, primarily composed of illiterate, poverty-stricken people whose only hope is escape from this "vale of tears" into a future where inequities disappear. We are involved in self-development and growth of talents that would have been submerged in other eras, and we recognize that continual inward molding as a lifelong, generation-spanning state of health. We want to be the yeast that makes the church itself able to encourage transformations that make this world fresh and alive.

We are searchers, constantly seeking and redefining God as we mature. We seek God who weaves spiritual direction into human intimacy and the interconnectedness of lives, who includes rather than excludes all people of good will regardless of gender, marital status, education, political persuasion, physical condition, age, or other culturally favored criteria of discrimination.

There is no other institution that discriminates and condescends to women as the institutional church does. We regret that. We affirm, however, our right to be here and to help build a supportive and stimulating community. We provide support to each other as we struggle to grow a church that addresses the depth and scope of spiritual hunger rather than merely counts the number of those who hunger.

We have many more possibilities to consider than our parents did: enough raw physical energy to blow the earth out of orbit; enough techniques to reshape life itself and make parenthood obsolete; enough diversity of lifestyles and modes of communication to drastically increase or decrease social tensions. We cannot just assimilate wisdom from the past. We must formulate new wisdom responsive to today's possibilities. Women ask that their church do no less.

*Doris Simonis*

Was I born inferior? Would God do that to us?

*Anon.*

I am a product of Catholic education in Cleveland, Toledo and St. Louis. I believe that education prepared me for this world, to live and work in it, for marriage and raising a Christian family. Besides the knowledge that those schools imparted, there was structure, caring discipline, examples of Christian living, and an understanding and appreciation of Holy Mother the church. As that education was important for me in the 1940s, 1950s and 1960s, it is even more important for young women in the new millennium. Mothers pass on to their children that which they feel is important and the church would be wise to recognize that.

*Sheila M. Nicholson*

Regarding women in the church, nothing less than proceeding to full membership and full privileges will do. In other areas, the church needs to work toward more democracy, with bishops being elected at least by the priests. Gays and lesbians should be encouraged to participate. There should be open ordination of gays because there is no reason to keep up the clandestine approach to what is already being done. Lastly, because of the strong secular influence via TV and movies today, the church needs to speak out very strongly for morality and ethics, and must continue to stress strong families and strong morals.

*Mary Hills*

~

I like men. They have been hunters and protectors. God gave us a uterus and ovaries so we could reproduce mankind. We can't totally blame men for the current situation. But men are perpetuating the system, especially the older guys. Changing the current situation should begin with younger men and women. But who can vote on change? Only the men! We're confronting a power structure here. It's the same type of power structure that existed at the Toledo Club, which used to be reserved only for men. That has now changed. There are even women on the board.

*Anon.*

~

My deep love for the church has been the basis for my over sixty years of religious life. The renewal of the church and of religious life called for by Vatican II only deepened my love. Many of its fruits can be seen in the vitality of parishes that "hung in"; in religious life and its transformation (U.S. women religious have undergone a process of transformation unlike any other corporate group in church history); in the renewed ministry of the laity; and in pockets of social awareness. But currently there is growing retrenchment from the vision of Vatican II, particularly regarding women's position in the church. While I rejoice in the articulation by Pope John Paul II of the social message of the gospel and his passionate call to fidelity to that message, I am saddened by what is transpiring in the internal life of the church. Therefore, I feel a responsibility to enter into loving critique.

Can American Catholic women hope that in the next century

there will be substantive changes necessary to ensure women equal and full participation in the life of the church? The answer appears negative if one looks to the current state of seminaries and recently ordained bishops. The official church constantly articulates an antiquated definition of the role of women in society, yet gives lip service to the need for women to hold position of leadership in the church, yet adamantly excludes them from the ministry of priesthood. This convoluted situation is deeply flawed. It manifests a fear on the part of leadership that they will lose the power of jurisdiction if they share it.

Let me clarify my own position. Though I had always longed for that moment when I could celebrate Eucharist, I with countless other women would not in conscience enter into priesthood as it is presently enfleshed. It is laden with such hierarchical layers that it fails, except in all too few cases, to engender any sense of the communal nature of the church and the priesthood of all the faithful who should actively participate in the decisions which affect its life.

Further, I believe that the present construct of ordained ministry militates against full human development. It is not the "men only" criteria for admission, but the denial of the right to marry. I fully believe in the freedom which celibacy represents, but I also know from long experience with priests that all too many of them are stunted in their development, and at times find themselves in relationships that are violations of their vows.

Despite these realities, what would I hope to see in the church?

1. Recognition of the theological currents flowing across the globe which include: a theology of human rights—and women's rights are human rights; a theology of liberation from every form of oppression, whether economic, social, political, cultural, or religious; a theology of feminism based on equality of persons; and a renewed theology of ecology, the planet being the footprint of God. All this would mean that the church be true to her own wonderful teaching about the dignity of the human person made in the image and likeness of God.

2. Recognition that God has been and is at work in religions other than Catholicism.

3. Recognition of the consistent ethic of life. Recent priority given to the anti-abortion agenda and the de-emphasis on the economic justice agenda is a misfortune. Food, clothing, shelter, education, employment at a living wage—these are all life issues. There are millions of children impoverished in our nation and globally while we spend increasing amounts to militarize our foreign policy. All too many Catholics adamantly focused on the "right to life" agenda have little understanding of the radical nature of the Gospel message which also includes the broader gamut of life issues.

4. Recognition that silencing dissenters is a violation of human dignity and right. It deprives the church of the wisdom that issues from dialogue and from loving critique which dissenters usually manifest.

I am at a point where I do not hope to see this change in my lifetime.

*A Woman Religious*

⌒

I thank the pope for his apology to women. We accept with gratitude this first step in amending wrongs that we have suffered. In this spirit, I would suggest that women be allowed to take their rightful place in the decision-making process of the church, both as laywomen and as clergywomen. I also ask that the language in prayers be amended to include women. Words have power and when one group is excluded this gives the impression that the group mentioned ("men") is superior. Further, I ask the church to assume a leadership role in educating men to the fact that women are not inferior. So much suffering comes from assuming women's inferiority. I am deeply moved by the pope's compassionate apology to all who have suffered because of the church and I am honored to be led by such a pope.

*Vincenza Dowling*

~

More and more Catholics are searching for a meaningful homily/sermon on Sunday, one that will carry them through the week. Many are "shopping" parishes to find this.

*Nancy Kennelly*

~

The real issue for me is one of equality: most decisions regarding the life of women, families, and communities ought to include women at all levels. To relegate decision-making, higher salaries, functions at worship, and positions of authority to males only amounts every day in every way to a continual, visible, active exclusion of women that no amount of pastorals will change. Our church should be a place that embodies the call to faith, hope, and love. Each person brings a different gift to the whole Body of Christ. Therefore, following the example of Jesus who loved the everyday people of his day into life and grace, all should be welcome. Women, the poor, the alien, homosexuals, peoples of diverse races, ethnic origins, and ages—all would be welcome.

Our church is not heaven but a hospital where all are welcome because all are in need of healing. As a living organism, the church is constantly called to conversion. Beginning with the official leadership of the church, sacrifices on behalf of the poor would be primary. I hope for a church that makes Mary's song real—our soul sings of our generous God who lifts up and feeds the lowly and sends away those who refuse to share with the poor.

*Christine Pratt, O.S.U.*

~

Women of the twenty-first century are more savvy, intelligent, secure, and productive than at any other time in history. The church needs to recognize this and begin to incorporate women's insights, opinions, and actions into issues that concern us all.

*Geneva Rodgers*

I envision a church in which women share completely in the culture, the tradition, and ritual life of the community of faith. Throughout the history of the church, women have ministered, supported, and challenged God's people. They have brought the message of the Gospel into the wider community, having an immeasurable impact on society. Women have served as leaders in education, healthcare, and social services. In this context, women have initiated a leadership style of participation and inclusivity that is directed by compassion and mutuality. This leadership model has challenged and stretched the development of our creativity while breaking down the competitive model that sets people at odds with one another. I dream of a church in which the value of women's contributions are acknowledged, treasured, and embraced.

*Shannon Schrein, O.S.F.*

What do I want for the church in the twenty-first century? I want a church that will appeal to my children. Not a permissive church, but a church that upholds its doctrine while being responsive to the needs of its members. A case in point is the Sunday sermon. This has the greatest impact on peoples' religious lives, but most priests are not great speakers. Most parishioners evaluate the Sunday sermons as very poor. Those in non-Catholic churches and on TV are far superior.

The Catholic church loses young people because of poor public relations and administrative policies rather than doctrine. I worry

about the future of my children. Half of them are no longer practicing Catholics. They have turned to other religions because the
ministers give inspiring sermons and are more responsive to their
needs.

*Lois Dupre Shuster*

We are discounted voices in the church. I don't want to work for
an organization that discounts me.

*Anon.*

Since the Second Vatican Council we have seen new doors open
for women to share their gifts in the church. Shown in Pope John
Paul II's apostolic letter "On the Dignity of Women," the church
has experienced a reawakening concerning the role of women. In
the light of Mary, woman of faith, the church marvels at the beauty
of women as mothers, religious, consecrated and singles.

I myself am thrilled to be giving of myself and living out the
missionary call of the church in the apostolate of religious education. In recent years I have also witnessed an increased recognition
of the dignity of motherhood. I have seen wives willingly sacrifice
careers for the love of their husband and children. Equally, I have
seen husbands lay down their lives for their children. When
women, like Mary, bear with sacrificial love for Christ, the entire
church is nourished. Families once again become "domestic
churches" and vocations to the priesthood increase. In light of this,
I believe that in the twenty-first century we will see more women
give of themselves in sacrificial love to the church.

*Elizabeth A. Riordan*

~

Women in America are articulate, educated, intelligent, spiritually grounded, and wise. The church in the twentieth century was
not equipped to cope with women such as we are. We were vital
participants in a democratic government but silenced in the most
important aspect of our lives—living the gospel values as Jesus
taught us. I look forward to the church in the twenty-first century
recognizing the strength and spirituality of the women of the
world. Allowing women greater participation in the teaching and
governmental structure of the church would heighten the rever-
ence members have for Mother church.

*Kathleen Padden, O.S.U.*

~

At meetings I attend with women, frustration is rampant. We
are dealing with the realization that within the decade we will not
have enough priests to minister to the needs of the faithful. In
many parishes that have collaborative pastors, women are already
pastoral associates, administrators, liturgists, and principals of our
schools. They manage the finances, physical plant and personnel,
minister to the sick and dying, counsel the wounded among us, as
well as those in financial and emotional need. They educate the
young, the adults, the unchurched, those contemplating marriage,
and those preparing to receive the sacraments. Yet in many
parishes, though women do the work, men are given the titles, the
salaries, the benefits.

In the twenty-first century, I hope that we as church learn to
value one another for our gifts, seeing past gender, race, disability,
sexual orientation, or anything that blocks our ability to affirm one
another as valuable. In God's eyes we are all His children. We are
ALL the body of Christ and need to function as one. If this does not
happen, there will be no church beyond the twenty-first century.

*Cecilia Roche*

# Epilogue

B Y WHAT RIGHT DO WOMEN SPEAK of their dreams for the church in the twenty-first century? They do not hold the authority of office. In many forums they are urged to practice the godly virtue of obedience to what the men in charge decide is right and true. If they criticize, it is often interpreted to mean a lack of allegiance that weakens the church already under threat from secular society. Yet around the world the voices of women are resounding with ever greater passion. Pondering what it means for women "to speak with the authority of the Spirit, whether recognized or not,"[1] the theologian Mary Catherine Hilkert turns for an answer to the witness of Catherine of Siena. Here is a fourteenth-century laywoman now publicly recognized as a saint and Doctor of the Church not only because of her holiness but also for her wisdom expressed through her "charism of exhortation." Fiercely loyal to the church, she nevertheless was an outspoken critic of its corruption. Possessing no theological degree or official mandate, she dared to advise popes and politicians about their duties. Her preaching trips were so successful that confessors were appointed to travel with her to deal with those whom she attracted to the gospel. Most tellingly, she signed her letters by invoking the name of the crucified Christ, his gentle mother, "and I Caterina." "What," Hilkert asks, "empowered this woman to speak and act with authority in the name of Christ?" How did she come to proclaim the truth so convincingly and unconventionally in the name of God's own heart, "mad with love" for hurting humanity? And, getting to the nub of the issue, "What inspiration can women, called to speak the truth of the gospel today, draw from her freedom, her

boldness, her fidelity, and her love of the broken body of Christ
and a wounded world?"[2]

Drawing liberally from Catherine's letters along with her mystical writings, Hilkert winnows the wheat from the time-conditioned
chaff. There is ultimately only one source of authority for the
church, namely, the Spirit of God who is love, fecundity, giver of all
life. Women in the fourteenth as well as the twenty-first centuries
are gifted with the Spirit in three ways:

- through their vocation as baptized persons that makes them
  into prophets, priests, and leaders as part of the body of Christ;

- through their actual experience of living the Christian life
  that gives them a growing wisdom in discerning the truth in
  love by the power of the Holy Spirit;

- through their negative contrast experiences of suffering, that
  makes them keenly aware of the power of sin and impels them
  to raise voices of resistance and hope in compassionate solidarity with those who weep.

The authority of vocation, of wisdom, of compassion—all three
arise from women's full participation in the life of the crucified
and risen Christ. In a word, women speak as persons of faith with
the authority of their experience of the quest for the living God.
Their deepest appeal is to the authority of the future when, in the
reign of God, the fullness of life, *shalom,* is poured out on everyone, the lowest and least most of all.

The conversations reflected in this book attempt to contribute
in a loving, peaceable, and at times critical way to the growing
strength of women's voices about matters of God in our own day.
"If these should keep quiet, the very stones would cry out" (Luke
19:40).

## NOTES

1. Mary Catherine Hilkert, *Speaking with Authority: Catherine of Siena
and the Voices of Women Today,* The Madeleva Lecture in Spirituality
(New York: Paulist Press, 2001), 7.

2. Ibid.

# Contributors

BARBARA HILKERT ANDOLSEN (Ph.D., Vanderbilt University) is Helen Bennett McMurray Professor of Social Ethics at Monmouth College, New Jersey.

SARA BUTLER, M.S.B.T. (Ph.D., Fordham University) is Professor of Systematic Theology at the University of St. Mary of the Lake, Mundelein, Illinois.

ANA MARÍA DÍAZ-STEVENS (Ph.D., Fordham University) is Professor of Church and Society at Union Theological Seminary at Columbia University in New York City.

MARY ANN GLENDON (J.D., University of Chicago) is the Learned Hand Professor of Law at Harvard University in Cambridge, Massachusetts.

COLLEEN GRIFFITH (Th.D., Harvard University) is Faculty Director of Spirituality Studies and Adjunct Assistant Professor of Theology in the Institute of Religious Education and Pastoral Ministry at Boston College.

DIANA HAYES (Ph.D., S.T.D., University of Louvain, Belgium) is Associate Professor of Systematic Theology at Georgetown University and Adjunct Professor at Xavier University's Institute of Black Catholic Studies and Howard Divinity School.

ELIZABETH JOHNSON, C.S.J. (Ph.D., Catholic University of America) is Distinguished Professor of Theology at Fordham University in New York City.

HON. MARCY KAPTUR (B.A., University of Wisconsin; Master's of Urban Planning, University of Michigan; doctoral studies, Massachusetts Institute of Technology) is a United States Congresswoman who has represented the ninth district of Toledo, Ohio, since 1983. She now ranks as senior Democratic woman in the U.S. House of Representatives.

SUSAN MUTO (Ph.D., University of Pittsburgh) is executive director of the Epiphany Association in Pittsburgh, Pennsylvania, a non-profit ecumenical center dedicated to spiritual formation, and co-founder of its Epiphany Academy of Formative Spirituality.

SISTER CATHERINE PATTEN, R.S.H.M. (Ph.D., New York University) is the coordinator of the Catholic Common Ground Initiative.

MIRIAM THERESE WINTER (Ph.D., Princeton Theological Seminary), a Medical Mission Sister, is Professor of Liturgy, Worship, Spirituality, and Feminist Studies and Director of the Women's Leadership Institute at Hartford Seminary in Hartford, Connecticut.

142

# Of Related Interest

ELIZABETH A. JOHNSON
**SHE WHO IS (Tenth Anniversary Edition)**
*The Mystery of God in Feminist Theological Discourse*

### WINNER OF THE LOUISVILLE
### GRAWEMEYER AWARD IN RELIGION!

"As perhaps the best book of feminist theology to date, *She Who Is* is at once thoroughly orthodox, grounded in classical Christian thought, liberatingly contemporary, and rooted in Women's experience."                                    —LIBRARY JOURNAL
0-8245-1925-6 $24.95, paperback

KATHY COFFEY
**DANCING IN THE MARGINS**
*Meditations for People Who Struggle with Their Churches*
From the acclaimed author of *Hidden Women of the Gospels,* this work richly demonstrates the plight of people within various religious traditions who are struggling with their churches. In response, Kathy Coffey generously offers interviews, poetry, Biblical reflections, and questions for reflection in the hopes of offering solace and solidarity to those still grappling with their church.
0-8245-1815-2, $14.95 paperback

KATHY COFFEY
**HIDDEN WOMEN OF THE GOSPELS**
"Can males profit from reading this book? I have. Its insights prompt understanding and prayer. The feminine perspective is enriching."                           —Jeremy Harrington, publisher,
ST. ANTHONY MESSENGER
0-8245-1561-7, $14.95, paperback

crossroad

# Of Related Interest

JOANNA MANNING
## IS THE POPE CATHOLIC?
*A Woman Confronts Her Church*

An outspoken advocate for women's equality, Joanna Manning powerfully articulates how John Paul II's current views on women are not only a problem for the Catholic Church, but also a threat to the well-being of all women, regardless of belief.

0-8245-1869-1, $18.95 paperback

PHYLLIS ZAGANO
## HOLY SATURDAY
*An Argument for the Restoration of the Female
Diaconate in the Catholic Church*

A serious effort to faithfully investigate the history and canonical viability of the female diaconate. Based on thorough research, as well as sound historical and theological analysis and reflection, this book makes a significant contribution to the discussion and development of women's roles in the modern church.

0-8245-1832-2, $16.95, paperback

BARBARA FIAND
## REFOCUSING THE VISION
*Religious Life into the Future*

"My last ten years' encounter with religious life, especially through my retreat and workshop ministry, has deeply enriched me, but has also increased my sense of urgency to bring things out into the open, to identify disagreements and encourage discussion, to invite us to come together in order to face the struggle that all of us are experiencing."

*—From the Preface*

0-8245-1890-X, $18.95 paperback

crossroad

# Of Related Interest

# Of Related Interest